PREPARE

WORKBOOK

B2

LEVEL 6

David McKeegan   Second Edition

Cambridge University Press
www.cambridge.org/elt

Cambridge Assessment English
www.cambridgeenglish.org

Information on this title: www.cambridge.org/9781108381192

© Cambridge University Press and Cambridge Assessment 2015, 2019

First published 2015
Second Edition 2019
20 19 18 17 16 15 14 13 12 11 10 9 8 7 6 5 4 3 2 1

Printed in Dubai by Oriental Press

A catalogue record for this publication is available from the British Library

ISBN 978-1-108-38119-2 Workbook with Audio Download
ISBN 978-1-108-43332-7 Student's Book
ISBN 978-1-108-38063-8 Student's Book and Online Workbook
ISBN 978-1-108-38598-5 Teacher's Book with Downloadable Resource Pack
(Class Audio, Video, Photocopiable Worksheets)

CONTENTS

1 NEW YEAR, NEW CHALLENGE

VOCABULARY   Education: phrasal verbs

1 Match the beginnings and ends of the sentences.

0	I enjoy trying	*c*	**a**	behind after school and do some extra work.
1	I think we break	....	**b**	down all the details in your book.
2	Daniel hasn't handed	....	**c**	out new things.
3	I'm going to go	....	**d**	up for the summer on 6th June.
4	Don't put things	....	**e**	out all the new assignments yesterday.
5	This year, I think I'm going to get	....	**f**	in his homework yet.
6	The swimming coach read	....	**g**	in the school football team this term.
7	I'm going to stay	....	**h**	out the answer to this maths problem.
8	Our teacher gave	....	**i**	out the names of everyone in the team.
9	I love joining	....	**j**	off for too long or you might never do them.
10	Don't forget to note	....	**k**	on well at school.
11	If I play well, I'll get	....	**l**	in when someone starts singing.
12	I can't figure	....	**m**	for the position of team captain.

2 Complete the email with the phrasal verbs in the box.

break up	figure out	get in	~~get on~~	give out	go for
hand in	join in	note down	put off	stay behind	try out

Hi Sophia,

I've just started at my new school and it's great. I think I'm going to ⁰ *get on* really well here. There are lots of interesting clubs – I'm going to ¹ .... rock climbing this year! I've never done it before, but it sounds fun so I decided to ² .... it.

The students in my class are really friendly. A few ³ .... after school to play basketball and they asked me to ⁴ .... with them. As you know, I'm pretty good at basketball and my new friends think I will ⁵ .... the school team if I try!

There's a lot more work to do, though. The teachers ⁶ .... homework every day and we have to ⁷ .... most of it the next morning. There's always one piece that we can do over the week, but I try not to ⁸ .... doing it for too long. I have to remember to ⁹ .... everything the teachers say about the homework, or I forget it. The timetable is quite complicated too, but I'll ¹⁰ .... where to go at what time soon, I'm sure!

We ¹¹ .... on 15th December, so I'll come and visit you then. Write soon!

Debbie

READING

1 What advice would you give to someone starting at a new school? Write three ideas.

....
....
....

2 Quickly read the article on page 5. Does the author give the same advice as you?

3 Match the headings to the paragraphs (A–G).

0	Get involved!	*F*
1	Find out about the school	....
2	Be a conversation starter	....
3	Don't be afraid to stand out	....
4	Pay attention to others	....
5	Be brave	....
6	Put on your friendly face	....

NEW KID *at school?*

Going to school in a new town can be pretty stressful. Believe me, I know from experience. Not to worry though, there are ways to get through it! Here are a few tips I've come up with. I hope they help!

A When you go in on your first day at your new school, remember that not everyone is as scary as they seem. Those first few hours are always a bit rough, but don't be afraid or shy. Just go for it! It's nearly always true that most people are nice once you have a chance to talk to them.

B It's likely that your teachers will introduce you to your new classmates, but make sure you personally introduce yourself to the student sitting next to you. Looking for something to talk about? Don't worry! Being new is a great topic. People seem to love talking about where you're from and the school you used to go to.

C Take time to learn the names of other people, and don't forget to take an interest in the person you're talking to. It shows that you're not just concerned about yourself, but also learning about the other person.

D It sounds obvious but it really works: make eye contact with others, smile at them when they look at you and laugh when they say something that's amusing to you. It makes you seem open and easy-going.

E Nobody expects you to know everything about your new school the first day you walk in. It's highly probable that your new school will be totally different from the one you just came from. If you have a question, ask it! Don't forget that everyone is new at some point.

F Whether you're entering a new school at the beginning of the year or in the middle, the best way to meet new people is by joining in activities like clubs and sports. After school is a time when students with similar interests get together and it's an ideal way to introduce yourself.

G If you're good at a certain sport or do well in a certain subject, don't be shy – show it! People are drawn to others with talent, and hiding yours to avoid showing off will only end up hurting you. So if you have a special talent or skill, let people know about it!

4 Complete the summary sentences.

0 People might seem scary at first, but *most people are nice when you talk to them.*

1 The fact that you are new can help you

2 It's a good idea to try to remember

3 You can let people know you are friendly by

4 You should ask questions about your new school because

5 The best way to meet new friends is

6 Don't be afraid to let others know if

5 Match the highlighted words and phrases in the text to the definitions.

1 attracted

2 perfect

3 think of (an idea or plan)

4 likely

5 difficult or unpleasant

1 Match the questions to the answers.

1 What clubs have you joined this term?
2 Were you getting ready to go out at 8.00 am this morning?
3 What team did you manage to get in last year?
4 Where do you usually go after school?
5 How have you changed since you were ten years old?
6 Can you swim 100 metres in less than two minutes?
7 Do you drink coffee at breakfast?
8 Should you spend longer on your homework in the evenings?

a The swimming team.
b Only the basketball and photography ones.
c No, I can't.
d I nearly always go straight home.
e Yes, I was.
f Yes, I probably should.
g No, never.
h I've grown much taller!

2 Put the words in the correct order to make questions.

0 you / lived / how long / in your house / have / ?
How long have you lived in your house?
1 go / you / did / on holiday / last year / ?

2 doing / at eight o'clock last night / you / were / what / ?

3 both / can / drive / your parents / ?

4 there / good cafés / are / near your school / any / ?

5 to do / going / you / are / tomorrow / what / ?

3 Choose the correct options to complete the subject and object questions.

0 Who (sits) / does sit next to you in class?
1 What watched you / did you watch on TV last night?
2 What means 'enrichment' / does 'enrichment' mean?
3 How that happened / did that happen to your bike?
4 Who called you / did call you during the science class?
5 What said you / did you say to the teacher?
6 Where like you / do you like going in the evenings?
7 Who ate / did eat all the chocolates?

4 Complete the questions.

0 How many _____ *cakes did you make* _____ ?
I made three cakes.
1 What sort of concerts _____ ?
Dan loves going to jazz concerts.
2 How many students _____ ?
At least 30 students joined the music club.
3 Who _____ ?
I phoned Jenny early this morning.
4 Who _____ ?
Martin phoned me early this morning.
5 What _____ ?
I think this word means 'difficult'.

5 Write one subject question and one object question for each situation.

0 Simon got in the swimming team.
Who got in the swimming team _____ ?
Simon.
What team did Simon get in _____ ?
The swimming team.
1 Steph does her homework before breakfast.
_____ ?
Steph.
_____ ?
Before breakfast.
2 My new bike cost €450.
_____ ?
€450.
_____ ?
My new bike.
3 Your sister gave me a bracelet for my birthday.
_____ ?
Your sister.
_____ ?
A bracelet.

6 Tick (✓) the correct sentences.

👁 0 A Why they are not here?
    B Why aren't they here?   ✓
1 A Is it still available in September?
   B Does it still available in September?
2 A Why it says this?
   B Why does it say this?
3 A Did you had a nice day?
   B Did you have a nice day?
4 A Why did she have to move?
   B Why she had to move?
5 A What language facilities you provide?
   B What language facilities do you provide?

1 Use the word given in capitals at the end of some of the lines to form a word that fits the gap in the same line.

My maths tutor	
Last year, I thought that maths was a subject which I would never be good at, so I didn't have any [0]*motivation* to improve. My	MOTIVATE
parents were worried, and decided to take [1]_____. They arranged a meeting with	ACT
the school head, who made the [2]_____	SUGGEST
that we should get a private maths tutor. I wasn't keen on the idea of extra school work, but after a long [3]_____ with my	DISCUSS
parents, I agreed to try it out. A week later, Mrs Feldman came to our house. My first [4]_____ was surprise. She was an older	REACT
lady, about the same age as my grandma. She had worked in [5]_____ all her life.	EDUCATE
Let me tell you, the way she taught was an [6]_____. She really brought the subject to	INSPIRE
life for me because her [7]_____ were so clear and lively.	EXPLAIN
Now, thanks to Mrs Feldman, I love maths so much that I've made the [8]_____ to study it at university!	DECIDE

2 Change the nouns to verbs. Then match the verbs to their definitions.

	noun	verb	definition
0	application	*apply*	*b*
1	concentration		
2	connection		
3	description		
4	definition		
5	explanation		
6	expression		
7	introduction		
8	invention		
9	permission		
10	preparation		
11	recommendation		
12	registration		

a put information, especially names, on an official list
b request something, usually officially
c allow
d design or create something which has never existed before
e say or write what something is like
f get someone or something ready for something that will happen
g make something exist, happen or be used for the first time
h join
i show what you think or how you feel using words or actions
j think very carefully about something you are doing and nothing else
k advise someone that something should be done
l make something clear or easy to understand
m explain the meaning of a word or phrase

1 Read the essay title. Add your own idea and notes in 1–3 for what you should write about.

'Sports should not be a compulsory subject in schools.' Do you agree?
Notes Write about:
1 the value of sports _____
2 the importance of other subjects _____
3 (your own idea) _____

2 Read the essay quickly. Are any of your ideas from Exercise 1 included? _____

1 Some people think that sport is an important part of life. it helps you to stay fit and healthy. Playing sport also teaches you things, like how to be part of a team, and the importance of hard work.

2 Other people might think that sport is not an important subject. They believe that school is for preparing people for the world of work. Very few people are good enough at sports to become professional, so they think its just a waste of time that could be spent on more important subjects.

3 This is an interesting question. I enjoy sport very much, but should it be a compulsory part of school education? Is it really necessary

4 So, I believe sport should be compulsory in schools. Not everyone will become a professional like the football player ronaldo, but that doesn't mean that we shouldn't try.

5 Personally, I think sport is fun! If you did nothing but study at school, it would become difficult to concentrate in lessons. Students would get bored very quickly

3 Read the essay again and match paragraphs 1–5 to a–e.

a *3* (introduction)   d ____ (your own idea)
b ____ (value of sports)   e ____ (conclusion)
c ____ (importance of other subjects)

4 There is one punctuation error in each of the paragraphs 1–5. Find and circle it.

5 Read the essay title. Add your own idea and notes in 1–3.

'School students should not have to do homework.' Do you agree?
Notes Write about:
1 the age of the student _____
2 how useful homework is _____
3 (your own idea) _____

6 Write your essay in 140–190 words. Use the five-paragraph plan in Exercise 3.

2 LIVE MUSIC

VOCABULARY Music phrases

1 Put the letters in the correct order to make types of music.

0	l a c s l i c a s	*classical*
1	k l o f	
2	p i p - h o h	
3	z a z j	
4	a r o p e	
5	g e r a g e	
6	c o r k	
7	o p p	

2 Match the words to make music phrases.

1	debut		**a**	the charts
2	in		**b**	the world
3	concert		**c**	album
4	massive		**d**	fans
5	go		**e**	hit
6	release		**f**	music
7	tour		**g**	singer
8	devoted		**h**	venue
9	lead		**i**	solo
10	give		**j**	talent
11	musical		**k**	a track
12	background		**l**	a performance

3 Complete the sentences with the words in the box.

background	charts	debut	fans	gave	hit
musical	released	singer	solo	toured	venue

1 I like their _____ album much better than their second one.
2 Their first single was a massive _____ all over the world.
3 Thousands of devoted _____ were waiting outside the stadium.
4 You've got a great voice. Do you want to be the lead _____ in my band?
5 I could never play an instrument because I have no _____ talent.
6 They're a successful band who have had several singles in the _____.
7 We _____ a few tracks online last year, but not many people downloaded them.
8 Ariana Grande _____ the world last year.
9 She _____ a great performance in London.
10 A football stadium is a great choice of concert _____ for popular artists.
11 The band split up and the members all went _____ in 2017.
12 You can still hear their songs everywhere, from TV ads to _____ music in lifts.

READING

1 Make a list of what steps are necessary to form a band. Then read the blog post on page 9 and check your ideas.

_____
_____
_____

2 Six sentences have been removed from the article. Choose from sentences A–G the one which fits each gap (1–6). There is one extra sentence which you do not need to use.

A That way you'll develop your own sound. ....
B You can usually hire these by the hour. ....
C Above all, enjoy yourself. ....
D Apart from that, motivation is the most important thing. ....
E The main thing to do, however, is to record a demo. ....
F But if you want to make it big, you need your own material. ....
G For me, that was the easy part. ....

3 Read the blog post again. Are the sentences *T* (True), *F* (False) or *NM* (Not Mentioned)? Correct the false sentences. Underline the parts of the text which tell you the answer.

0 It is difficult to find people to play in your band.
F. A lot of people want to be in a band.

1 It's OK to be influenced by other bands' styles.
_____

2 The best songs are usually created by the whole band.
_____

3 You may have to pay for a room to practise in.
_____

4 The best way to make money is to play concerts.
_____

5 It's good to use studio time to practise your songs.
_____

6 Make friends with people doing the same sort of thing as you.
_____

How to
START YOUR OWN BAND

A lot of readers have been asking me for advice about how to put a band together, so I thought it was time to write a post about my experience. Every band has a different story, but hopefully some of the stuff below will be useful to you.

First, you've got to choose your band members. 1 _____ I was at college with a great bunch of musicians, so I didn't have to look far. You might not be so lucky, but there are all sorts of other ways to find members. In fact finding musicians isn't as hard as you think, as a lot of people want to be in a band. You can place ads in local colleges, music shops, or even the local press if you're willing to pay. Or just ask around – friends, friends of friends. Do make it clear which musicians you're looking for though, so that you don't waste people's time. Drummers are always the hardest to find!

It's important that you play the music that feels right to you. Don't just go for what's popular at the time – you need to play what you love. Your favourite bands and their styles will obviously be an influence on you, and that's fine. However, you need to do something a bit different. Don't just copy them! Mix and match until you find a sound you all like. 2 _____

You don't have to write your own songs. Some bands just play other people's songs all the time, and are quite happy with that. 3 _____ Not everyone has the musical talent for this, but if one or more of you in the group do, you're in luck. Maybe one of you has a tune they created. Any of you can suggest ideas, and you can all use this as a base to build on. Keep it simple at first, and you'll get there eventually.

Finding a good place to practise is essential. There has to be enough space for the band and all the gear, plus it has to be somewhere where the noise won't bother other people too much. A garage can be good, as long as there isn't a car in it. Some towns and villages have community rooms that you can use. 4 _____ Take your time to have a look around. You'll find somewhere eventually.

When you're good enough, you'll want to promote your band and start looking for gigs. Setting up a website is easy nowadays, and you can do it for free. 5 _____ This will cost you, as you will need to book time in a studio. Get your songs as near perfect as possible beforehand, because studio time is expensive. Three or four should be fine – then upload them to your website so people can hear what you've got.

When you get your first gig, try to produce some promotional stuff – T-shirts, badges, that kind of thing. They get your name 'out there', and most bands make more money doing that than from playing live at the beginning. Work hard, practise and keep writing new songs. Play at local venues and get to know other bands in your area – all contacts are good contacts. 6 _____ Whether or not you ever make the big time, being in a band is an experience worth having that you'll remember all your life.

1 Choose the correct options to complete the conversations.

1 A: What's the name of that song you *play* / *'re playing* now? It *sounds* / *'s sounding* great!

   B: It's called *Three Little Birds*. *Do you want* / *Are you wanting* me to teach it to you?

2 A: Where is Dana? I *don't see* / *haven't seen* her for hours.

   B: She *runs* / *'s running* in the park. She always *goes* / *is going* for a run on Sundays.

   A: I should do something like that. Running *keeps* / *is keeping* you fit.

3 A: *Do you go* / *Are you going* to the concert at the Rialto tonight?

   B: I *don't know* / *'m not knowing*. Who *plays* / *'s playing*?

   A: The Creds. They *are* / *have been* on tour since May.

   B: Mmm, I *don't like* / *'m not liking* The Creds.

4 A: *Have you still sung* / *Are you still singing* in that band?

   B: What, the one at school? Yes, I *'m* / *'ve been* with them for nearly a year now.

   A: *Have you done* / *Do you do* any concerts recently?

   B: Yes, quite a few. In fact, we *play* / *'re playing* one tomorrow evening. Why don't you come?

2 Write sentences using the correct present tense.

0 I / go / to a concert / this weekend
I'm going to a concert this weekend.

1 He / always / have / a burger before / he / play

2 Donna / seem / enjoy / dancing

3 You / do / lots of exercise / today

4 I / love / this band / since before they were famous

5 You / need / practise / to be any good

6 Kerry / not / understand / why / her friends / love / hip-hop

7 Pablo / learn / how to play / the piano / at the moment

8 Claudia and her band / write / several new songs / since their last concert

3 Complete the email with the verbs in brackets in the correct present tense.

Hi guys

I ¹＿＿＿＿＿＿＿ (think) about booking a couple of hours at the recording studio next week so we can make our demo. I ²＿＿＿＿＿＿＿ (need) to know what day and time everyone can make it. We all ³＿＿＿＿＿＿＿ (go) to school every day, so it ⁴＿＿＿＿＿＿＿ (have to) be an evening or Saturday. Danny ⁵＿＿＿＿＿＿＿ (have) driving lessons every Monday and Wednesday night, and I ⁶＿＿＿＿＿＿＿ (do) karate on Tuesdays and Thursdays – so that leaves Friday or Saturday.

Ava, ⁷＿＿＿＿＿＿＿ (you / go) to Jake's party on Friday? If not, let's try for that day.

The studio ⁸＿＿＿＿＿＿＿ (cost) €80 an hour, but that's OK. We ⁹＿＿＿＿＿＿＿ (be) together as a band for six months now, and I ¹⁰＿＿＿＿＿＿＿ (think) we're ready.

Got to go now – Dad ¹¹＿＿＿＿＿＿＿ (cook) dinner and ¹²＿＿＿＿＿＿＿ (want) me to lay the table. Call me!

Steve

4 Correct the mistakes in four of the sentences. Which two are correct?

1 The older dancers are teaching our traditional dance classes every week.

2 I am writing to complain about your report concerning the music festival.

3 Like everyone, I had some embarrassing moments in my life.

4 In both restaurants they play calm, melodious music, which creates a nice atmosphere.

5 They're very popular and they're playing very good music.

6 I have very broad experience of organising summer camps because I am working in summer camps for foreign schoolchildren for about ten years.

Verb + infinitive/-ing with a change in meaning

1 Match the sentences to their meanings in each pair.

1 I tried running, but I soon got bored.
2 I tried to run, but my coat was trapped in the door.

A it was difficult
B it was an experiment

3 We stopped to get something to eat.
4 We stopped eating and got in the car.

A it was the reason we stopped
B the activity stopped

5 He remembered locking the door.
6 He remembered to lock the door.

A he didn't forget to do the action
B he recalled the action

7 I forgot to go to the internet café.
8 I'll never forget going to an internet café for the first time.

A I will remember the experience
B I didn't remember to do the action

2 Complete the sentences with the correct form of the verbs in the box.

lock	reach	talk	turn	watch	win

1 Jake forgot _____ his bike when he went into the shop, and it was gone when he came out.
2 My aunt Becky is lovely but she's quite tiring to be with because she never stops _____!
3 A: I can't get this TV to work.
  B: Have you tried _____ it off and on again?
4 I'll always remember Spain _____ the World Cup in 2010.
5 Lucy was trying _____ the biscuits at the top of the cupboard when she fell off the chair.
6 We were driving home but it was such a beautiful evening that we stopped _____ the sunset.

1 You will hear five people talking about their experiences at a music festival. Tick (✓) the topics you think they will talk about.

1 the music _____
2 camping at the festival _____
3 the food _____
4 the weather _____
5 safety _____
6 comedy acts _____
7 prices _____
8 staff at the festival _____
9 parking _____
10 communications _____

2 Read the statements A–H and underline the key words.

A It was more expensive than I expected.
B I learned a lot about other cultures.
C The wide variety of bands performing was impressive.
D It was quite hard to find my way around.
E I regularly go to events like this.
F It was easy to keep in touch with my friends.
G I was surprised by the high quality of the facilities.
H The music made it difficult to sleep at night.

3 Listen to five people talking about their experiences at a music festival. Choose from the list (A–H) in Exercise 2 what each person says about the experience. There are three extra statements which you do not need to use.

Speaker 1 _____
Speaker 2 _____
Speaker 3 _____
Speaker 4 _____
Speaker 5 _____

4 Listen again and check your answers in Exercise 1.

3 FAMILY MATTERS

1 Use the clues below to complete the crossword with verbs of communication.

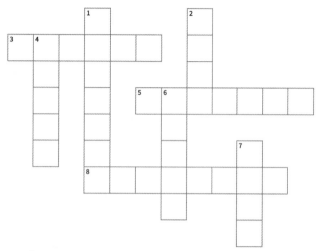

Across
3 Don't … me of being lazy. I'm just really tired today.
5 Donna will never … to doing anything wrong.
8 Did the teacher … to keep everyone in after class? He often does that.

Down
1 I … you spend more time studying and less time playing games.
2 I forgot to … you not to leave your bike outside.
4 Harry didn't … to be an expert – he just said he'd played the game before.
6 I'm not going to … you to do anything – you only have to do it if you want to.
7 It's obvious that you didn't enjoy my story, so don't try to … it.

2 Choose the correct verbs to complete the sentences.
1 I completely *deny / confess / accuse* dropping your laptop.
2 Conor *threatened / suggested / claimed* that they all go to the cinema.
3 I'm *ordering / denying / warning* you – it's dangerous to walk through the park at night.
4 My mum *threatened / accused / suggested* to sell our games console if we didn't help her with the housework.
5 You have been *warned / denied / accused* of a very serious crime.
6 OK, OK, I *deny / confess / order* to not going to school this morning.
7 The teacher *threatened / ordered / suggested* the whole class to stay behind after school.
8 Are you *claiming / warning / accusing* that the dog ate your homework?

3 Rewrite the sentences using verbs from Exercise 1.

I'll stop your pocket money if you don't tidy your room.

0 Dad *threatened to stop my pocket money.*

No, I did not eat the last piece of cake!

1 Sara ....

You broke the window, didn't you, Tom?

2 Mum ....
....

Don't play football in the street, kids – it's dangerous.

3 The police officer ....
....

Why don't we download that new comedy film?

4 Jack ....

1 Can you think of any famous brothers and sisters, either modern-day or from history?

....

2 Quickly read the four short biographies on page 13 and match them to the pictures (A–D).

Famous **brothers** and **sisters**

The Brontës

Picture _____

In the mid-19th century, three English sisters, Emily, Charlotte and Anne, [0] *made* a huge impression on the literary world. [1] _____ they were children, the three girls, and their brother Branwell, used to create fictional worlds together. They were inspired [2] _____ twelve wooden soldiers which their father had given them. Their first stories were written in tiny books of about 4 x 6.5 cm in size – just the [3] _____ size for the little soldiers to read.

They continued to write poems and stories into adulthood. Then, in 1847, all three sisters [4] _____ novels published – and they were a great success. [5] _____, as it was considered very unusual for women to publish books in [6] _____ days, they all used men's names. Not [7] _____ their publishers knew their true identities. In fact, one publisher at the time believed the novels were all the [8] _____ of one man!

The Wright brothers

Picture _____

Brothers Wilbur and Orville Wright are famous for inventing the first aeroplane. Their interest in flight started on the day their father brought home a toy helicopter for them. It was made of paper and wood, and was powered by a rubber band. The boys played with it until it broke, and then made their own to replace it. Although they were very clever, neither of them finished high school.

When they were older, they owned a bicycle shop where they started manufacturing and selling their own bikes. It became very successful and provided them with the money to pay for their experiments in flight. Eventually, they built their first 'flying machine'. Although it worked very well, it took several years before any government or business took them seriously enough to give them any money!

HAIM

Picture _____

The three sisters Alana, Danielle and Este Haim grew up in California. They got their love of music from their parents and spent much of their childhood listening to the classic rock records from the 1970s which they owned. Their musical careers started while they were still at school, when their parents formed a family band. They used to play at charity fairs but they never made much money.

In 2006, the girls decided to form their own band. They played at local venues but because all three sisters were doing other things, they did not take the band too seriously. After Este graduated in 2010, Danielle finished high school and Alana left college, they released three songs as a free download on their website. Since then, they have become one of the United States' most successful pop bands.

The Williams sisters

Picture _____

When you think of famous sporting sisters, the first names to spring to mind are Venus and Serena. The Williams sisters grew up in a poor area of Los Angeles, where their father Richard taught them to play tennis. He used what he had learned from books and videos to coach them. When she was only ten years old, Venus – the older of the two – could serve the ball at speeds of over 160 km/h! However, Serena is now generally regarded as the better of the two players.

The sisters entered the professional tennis circuit in their early teens, and soon began to dominate the game. Between them they have won dozens of titles – often playing against each other in the finals. But, in spite of their competitive natures, they remain very close. In fact, they share a house in Florida.

---

3 Read the text about the Brontës again and think of the word which best fits in each gap (1–8). Use only one word in each gap.

4 According to the four biographies, which of the brothers/sisters …

1 were influenced by their parents' tastes?

2 were inspired by a childhood gift?

3 won prizes?

4 didn't have a complete education?

5 were successful before they became adults?

6 worked together to produce something artistic?

5 Match the highlighted words in the texts to the definitions.

1 wanting very much to win or be more successful than other people

2 producing in large numbers, usually in a factory using machines

3 began to exist or made something begin to exist

4 provided with energy and the ability to operate

5 be more important, powerful or successful than other people

1 Choose the correct options to complete the texts.

1 When I ^a *was / had been* a little girl, I ^b *was getting / used to get* really excited about getting on a bus. Then I ^c *started / had started* school and I ^d *had / was having* to take the bus every day. It's not so exciting any more.

2 We ^a *didn't have / weren't having* much money this time last year. My dad ^b *was working / had worked* in a shoe factory and my mum ^c *was being / was* a waitress. Then, in January this year, we ^d *watched / were watching* TV in the living room when Dad ^e *came / had come* home and ^f *was telling / told* us he ^g *was winning / had won* six million euros!

3 **A:** What *had you done / were you doing* at ten o'clock last night?
B: I *slept / was sleeping*. It *had been / was being* a long, hard day.

2 Match the beginnings and ends of the sentences.

1 Once I had finished my homework, ...
2 I was walking home from school ....
3 I used to watch a lot of Disney movies ....
4 I picked up my phone ....
5 When I was a little baby, ...
6 I hadn't heard the door bell ....

a and texted my friend Rachel.
b my mother used to sing to me.
c when I saw the bus crash into the wall.
d I went to the park to play football.
e but I don't now.
f so I was surprised to find a parcel on the floor outside.

3 Complete the text with the correct past tense form of the verbs in the box. Sometimes more than one answer is possible.

be	break	enjoy	fill	finish
forget	jump	laugh	lie	walk

When we ¹ .... young kids, my brother and I ² .... playing tricks on each other. Making my brother jump in fright was my favourite trick. I ³ .... for ages when I did that!
One sunny day, my brother ⁴ .... on the grass in the garden sunbathing, just near the back door, which was made of glass. We ⁵ .... just .... school for the day, so it was about 3.30 in the afternoon. I went to the kitchen and ⁶ .... a large cup full of water. Then I ⁷ .... quietly towards the garden, on my toes, intending to jump out of the doorway and surprise him with a face full of water. Instead, I ⁸ .... straight into the back door, and ⁹ .... my nose on the hard glass. I ¹⁰ .... to open the door!

4 Correct the mistakes in four of the sentences. Which one is correct?

1 I remember the times we were going to the sea.
....

2 When they arrived at the bus stop, a big birthday cake was waiting for them.
....

3 He saw that the door is broken.
....

4 When we went to the beach, we use to swim all day.
....

5 I had visited the festival last weekend and I greatly enjoyed it.
....

1 Complete the second sentence so that it has a similar meaning to the first sentence, using the word given. Do not change the word given. You must use between two and five words, including the word given.

1 My brother and I had an argument and now we're not talking.
FELL
I .... my brother, and now we're not talking.

2 She never understood or shared the feelings of her older sister.
IDENTIFY
She couldn't .... her older sister.

3 Why is Adam treated so unfairly by everyone?
PICK
Why .... Adam?

4 I will always help you if you need me.
DEPEND
You can always .... help you.

5 She managed to persuade her uncle to take her to the match.
TALKED
She .... her to the match.

6 His father is very different to him.
TAKE
He .... his father.

1 Read the email. Why is Marie writing to Jack?

a to make a suggestion
b to ask for advice
c to give an opinion

Hi Jack!

I'm writing to you because I have a family problem. As I told you, I've got two younger brothers – Dan, who's 12, and Eric, who's eight. The trouble is, Dan is always picking on Eric. My parents don't seem to notice. How can I stop him doing that? I know you have brothers. What would you do?

Cheers,

Marie

---

2 Quickly read Jack's reply. What does he suggest?

....
....

⁰Dear Marie,

Thanks for your email. ¹It's a pleasure to hear from you!

I am sorry to hear about your problem. It is a difficult one because you want to stop Dan picking on Eric, but you do not want to ²damage your relationship with Dan. So you have got to be careful. My own brothers sometimes fight, and I always think the answer is to communicate with each other.

³My suggestion to you is that you speak to Dan privately. Explain to him that he is making Eric unhappy, and that this is making you unhappy, too. ⁴Another possible solution is asking Dan to try to ⁵identify with Eric. He would not like to be picked on by someone older and bigger than him, would he?

Anyway, that is enough from me. I hope this helps with your problem. Let me know how things turn out.

⁶Yours sincerely,

Jack

---

3 Jack's email sounds very formal. Match the highlighted words and phrases in the email to the informal words and phrases in the box. Write them below.

fall out   It's great   Take care   You might want to understand how it feels to be   Hi   Or how about

0	Hi	2	....	4	....	6	....
1	....	3	....	5	....		

4 Read Jack's email again. Change the verbs to their contracted forms, where possible. Write them below.

I am – I'm

....
....

5 You have received an email from your English-speaking friend. Write your answer in 140–190 words.

Hi!

I'm writing to you for some advice. The problem is, my parents are so strict with me! I always have to be home before 10.30 pm, and I'm never allowed to stay the night at a friend's house. I think I should be given more freedom, now that I'm 16. How much freedom do your parents give you? I'm sure they're not so strict. What do you think I should do?

Hope you can help!

Mia

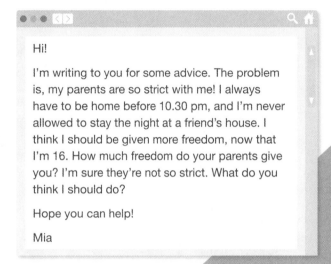

4 FORCES OF NATURE

VOCABULARY — Natural disasters: verbs

1 Label the picture with the verbs in the box.

| collapse | crack | drag | erupt | float | knock over | run | shake | smash |

2 Write sentences describing the things in the picture using the verbs in Exercise 1.

0 building	*The building is shaking.*
1 ground	
2 volcano	
3 lava / down / side / volcano	
4 car / lamppost	
5 man / sofa	

3 Complete the sentences with the correct form of the verbs in Exercise 1.

1 The suitcase was too heavy to lift, so I .... it to the car.

2 Our kitchen was flooded because someone had left the tap ....

3 The city of Pompeii was destroyed when a volcano .... in 79 CE.

4 A hot-air balloon .... over our house this morning.

5 The window .... when the stone hit it, but it didn't break completely.

6 Every time a train went past our tent, the ground ....

7 He was so heavy that the chair .... under his weight.

8 I wasn't looking where I was going and I accidentally .... an old lady.

9 She .... the bottle into tiny pieces by throwing it against the wall.

READING

1 Quickly read the article on page 17. What's the most dangerous type of tornado?

....

2 Read the first two paragraphs of the article again. Decide which answer (A, B, C or D) best fits each gap.

0	**A** tells	**B** says	**C** speaks	**D** talks
1	**A** word	**B** sentence	**C** statement	**D** expression
2	**A** origin	**B** start	**C** birth	**D** beginning
3	**A** thought	**B** known	**C** believed	**D** understood
4	**A** brand	**B** kind	**C** species	**D** sort
5	**A** explain	**B** express	**C** excuse	**D** expose
6	**A** take	**B** bring	**C** hold	**D** pick
7	**A** actually	**B** directly	**C** immediately	**D** eventually
8	**A** still	**B** even	**C** more	**D** yet

(0 B is circled)

INCREDIBLE TORNADOES

Nobody really ⁰ _says_ it any more, but you've probably heard the old-fashioned English ¹ _____ 'It's raining cats and dogs' to describe very heavy rain. The ² _____ of this idiom is obscure, and it has almost certainly never happened in real life. However, many other surprising things have been ³ _____ to rain down from the clouds. One morning in 1981, the citizens of Naphlion, in Greece, saw small green frogs falling from the sky. They landed in trees, on roofs and on the streets. The ⁴ _____ of frog came from North Africa, hundreds of kilometres away!

The phenomenon is quite easy to ⁵ _____ : small whirlwinds or tornadoes may form in certain weather conditions, which can ⁶ _____ up small things – creatures or objects – when they pass over water. These can then be carried for many kilometres, and ⁷ _____ , they will be dropped by the clouds carrying them. There have been reports of fish, tomatoes, and ⁸ _____ rocks, being dropped from the sky.

However, it seems that fish are the most common thing to fall from the clouds (apart from rain). They are the lightest and most common inhabitants of water, after all. In one town in Honduras, a 'Rain of Fish' happens every year. The people of the area even have a festival to celebrate the occasion.

These stories tend to make light of the true nature of tornadoes, though. They are a force of nature that can be truly terrifying. There are many types of tornado and while most are relatively harmless, like the ones described above, every year parts of the world experience huge tornadoes, which can bring extreme destruction. They have been known to destroy whole towns, and kill thousands of people. And worse, some of them can be made of fire!

Known as 'fire tornadoes,' they usually occur when a large wildfire is in progress. These fires are so hot that they can create their own wind, which can turn into a spinning whirlwind of flame. Under the right conditions, they can grow to over ten metres wide and 300 metres tall. Although fire tornadoes usually move quite slowly, they can cause an incredible amount of destruction. They will set anything in their way on fire and throw burning objects into the surrounding areas. Sometimes they can last for more than an hour, and it is impossible to put them out. You just have to wait.

Glen Mason is one man who saw a fire tornado close up. He watched it for over half an hour before it finally died. 'It was about 500 metres away and it sounded just like a jet plane,' he said. 'It was terrifying, but also the most amazing and exciting thing I've ever seen. I'm a very lucky man – both to have seen it and to have survived it!'

3 Read the whole article again. Are the sentences _T_ (True), _F_ (False) or _NM_ (Not Mentioned)? Correct the false sentences.

1 It is not known where the phrase 'It's raining cats and dogs' comes from.

2 In Naphlion, people were surprised to see rocks falling from the sky.

3 Objects are picked up from the water by clouds.

4 People have been killed by rocks falling from the sky.

5 Fire tornadoes are not so dangerous when they move slowly.

6 Glen Mason is glad that he experienced a fire tornado.

4 Match the highlighted words and phrases in the article to the definitions.

1 people or animals that live in a particular place _____

2 in a position around something _____

3 something that exists or happens, usually something unusual _____

4 not able or not likely to cause danger or damage _____

5 turning around very quickly _____

1 Choose the correct options to complete the sentences.

0 That is _B_ the most amazing thing I have ever seen.
   A slightly   B easily   C far
1 My computer is a ____ deal faster than yours.
   A quite   B good   C big
2 Volcanoes are ____ more terrifying than thunderstorms.
   A good   B quite   C far
3 My little sister is ____ as tall as me.
   A slightly   B almost   C a good deal
4 This medicine has made me feel ____ worse.
   A easily   B not quite   C a good deal
5 The more you practise, ____ you will become.
   A the best   B the better   C the good
6 Can I have a ____ larger piece of cake, please?
   A slightly   B easily   C quite
7 My grade was not ____ as good as I expected.
   A almost   B easily   C quite

2 Complete the sentences with the adjectives in brackets. Use the … the … .

0 _The larger_ asteroids are, _the easier_ they are to see. (large / easy)
1 My grandfather says _____ you get, _____ it becomes to change. (old / hard)
2 _____ the weather, _____ my sister is. (hot / happy)
3 _____ you are, _____ it is to ride your bike. (sleepy / dangerous)
4 _____ it got, _____ it became. (late / dark)
5 _____ you wait, _____ it will become to do anything. (long / difficult)

3 Complete the second sentence so that it means the same as the first sentence. Use the word in brackets.

0 That's the scariest film I've ever seen, by far. (easily)
   That's _easily the scariest film_ I've ever seen.
1 A rhinoceros is not quite as big as an elephant. (slightly)
   An elephant _____ rhinoceros.
2 Tonya is not quite as clever as Kaye. (almost)
   Tonya _____ as Kaye.
3 That party was much more interesting than I expected. (a good deal)
   That party _____ than I expected.
4 You'll need to study a good deal harder if you want to succeed. (far)
   You'll need to _____ if you want to succeed.
5 Mr Andrews is much stricter than Ms Knight. (a lot less)
   Ms Knight is _____ than Mr Andrews.

4 Tick (✓) the correct sentences.

1 A It was far worse from all the other storms that I had experienced.
   B It was far worse than all the other storms that I had experienced.
2 A The hotel is much more cheaper, and they have good bar food.
   B The hotel is much cheaper, and they have good bar food.
3 A As much as you study, as much as you will improve your English.
   B The more you study, the more you will improve your English.
4 A I hope we don't have many more earthquakes this year.
   B I hope we don't have much more earthquakes this year.

1 Choose the correct words to complete the sentences.

1 It was *so / too* hot outside that you could fry an egg on the pavement.
2 It was *so / such* a strong wind that I had to get off my bike and walk.
3 It's much *so / too* risky to swim in this river.
4 There are *so / such* many things to see in this city that it would take weeks to see them all.
5 This coffee is far *too / such* cold to drink – I'm sending it back.
6 It was *so / such* a funny film that my sides hurt by the end of it.
7 That restaurant is far *so / too* expensive to eat in every week.
8 I'm *so / such* happy that I could dance!

2 Rewrite the sentences with too, so or such.

0 You have such lovely eyes that I want to paint them. (so)
   Your eyes are so lovely that I want to paint them.
1 The book was too boring to finish. (such)
   _____
2 The exam was so hard that nobody got a good mark. (too)
   _____
3 She's such a kind person that everyone loves her. (so)
   _____
4 We arrived late so we couldn't see the film. (too)
   _____
5 The weather was so bad that we never left the hotel all holiday. (such)
   _____

1 Label the photos (A–D) with the words in the box.

> earthquake   flood   volcano   wildfire

🔊 02 **2** Listen to four news reports. Match the topic of each news report to a photo in Exercise 1.

1 _____   2 _____   3 _____   4 _____

🔊 02 **3** Listen again and complete the journalists' notes with one or two words or numbers.

1

Time of earthquake: [1] _____
Length of earthquake: [2] _____
seconds
Year of previous big earthquake:
[3] _____

2

Large volcanic [4] _____
on island of Morania
People trying to escape [5] _____
running down mountain
Danger of complete [6] _____

3

This is the [7] _____ time this
has happened recently
Water [8] _____ through the streets
of Bigham
People angry at [9] _____

4

Number of homes destroyed:
over [10] _____
Firefighting made difficult by
[11] _____
Number of injured: [12] _____

4 Answer the questions about the four news reports.

1 In 1, why are people afraid to return to their houses?
_____

2 In 2, how are people escaping from the island?
_____

3 In 3, why are people in the village of Bigham angry?
_____

4 In 4, what do people think caused the disaster?
_____

A _____

B _____

C _____

D _____

5 VIRTUAL ACTION

1 Use the definitions to complete the crossword with video gaming verbs.

Across
1 build something from several parts
4 move smoothly over a surface
6 talk and do things with other people
7 collect several things, often from different places or people
8 make a vehicle move more slowly or stop
11 be in a position where you will not fall to either side
12 drive a vehicle backwards

Down
2 go past a vehicle or person that is going in the same direction
3 move quickly, often to avoid something
4 control the direction of a vehicle
5 give something to someone and receive something similar from them
9 move somewhere by turning in a circular direction
10 run after someone or something in order to catch them

2 Choose the correct verbs to complete the sentences.

1 Let's go out and *chase / gather* some flowers from the garden.
2 This bike is so heavy that it is hard to *steer / brake* in the right direction.
3 I *balanced / dived* behind a wall when I heard the car approaching.
4 You have to *construct / interact* a city in this game.
5 How long can you *balance / roll* on one foot for?
6 An angry dog *chased / braked* me on the way home last night.
7 I prefer games which allow you to *interact / chase* with other players.
8 Do you want to *balance / exchange* this computer for a bike?
9 The Ferrari's going too slowly – why doesn't he *overtake / reverse* it?
10 When I fell off my skateboard, it *rolled / chased* to the bottom of the hill without me.
11 He won't be able to drive forwards into that parking space – he'll have to *overtake / reverse*.
12 If she doesn't *brake / gather* soon, she'll crash on the next corner.
13 He *balanced / slid* the plate across the table and I picked it up.

1 Look at the covers of the three video games. Which do you think would be the most fun to play?

JIMMY'S GAME REVIEWS

A ROCKET RACE picture ____ ⭐⭐

Rocket Race is the latest game from the highly successful SpeedCo games producer. They have produced every racing game imaginable, from racing cars to horses – but this is the first time they have left planet Earth!

As you can probably guess, it's all about racing rockets – and it's great fun! You have full control over the design of your vehicle, which you then construct and race against a team of other pilots. There is a choice of over twenty different race routes that take you round spectacular planets, asteroids and other parts of the universe. The graphics are truly superb.

The only criticism I have of the game is the music. I don't know who decided a rock soundtrack was a good idea, but it's not what I would choose. I think it sounds dreadful!

But overall, it's a really good game – especially for children as it's quite easy – and I'd certainly recommend it to anyone who enjoys racing games and outer space.

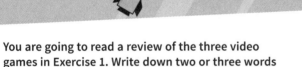

B BATTLE FIRE GALAXY picture ____ ⭐

You might think that the games market doesn't need another fantasy role-playing game, but Middle Earth Games have other ideas. This game sends you to find the magic Ring of Argor. You'll have endless adventures on the way, avoiding traps, picking up friends and weapons, and, of course, battling monsters.

There are ten levels to complete and as you go through them, you become more and more powerful. This is good, because the levels get more and more difficult to finish. It's challenging, but that's what you'd expect from this producer of intelligent games.

I do think that the graphics could be improved, though. They looked a bit old-fashioned to me, which made the game less enjoyable. The accompanying music wasn't so great, either.

This is really a game for fans of fantasy role plays. To an experienced gamer, it doesn't really offer anything new. It's OK as far as it goes, but it doesn't go very far.

C NATION BUILDER picture ____ ⭐⭐⭐

Have you ever wanted to be the ruler of your own country? With *Nation Builder*, the latest release from AceGamesUK, you can. But watch out – it's not as easy as it looks!

You start with nothing – just a field in the middle of nowhere – and build from there. Gathering building materials is your first job, as you have to make a house of some kind before night, when your enemies come out. If you can't protect yourself from them, you have to start again. The longer you survive, the more people come to live with you and cooperate with you in the war against your enemies. Eventually you have your own nation.

I can't think of anything bad to say about this game! It's packed with great features: the graphics are good, the way you build your nation is really clever, and the possibilities are only limited by your own imagination.
Not only is it great fun, but you learn a lot about the day-to-day running of a country.

Seriously, I can't recommend this game highly enough. Buy it!

2 **You are going to read a review of the three video games in Exercise 1. Write down two or three words that you might find in each one.**

1 ....
2 ....
3 ....

3 **Read the video game reviews and match them to the correct pictures in Exercise 1. Check your answers to Exercise 2.**

4 **Tick (✓) the correct video game A, B or C for each question. Sometimes more than one answer is possible. <u>Underline</u> the parts of the text which tell you the answer.**

Which game …

	A	B	C
1 gets the best review?			
2 gets the worst review?			
3 does not have good music?			
4 has the best graphics?			
5 has the worst graphics?			
6 is educational?			
7 involves fighting?			
8 is surprisingly difficult?			
9 is the least difficult?			
10 has no original ideas?			

5 **Match the highlighted words in the texts to the definitions.**

1 the music used in a film, TV programme or video game ....
2 objects used in fighting or war, such as guns, swords, etc. ....
3 when you say that something or someone is bad ....
4 a game, book or musical recording that is made available to buy ....
5 continue to live ....

GRAMMAR Relative clauses

1 Complete the sentences with *who*, *which*, *whose* or *where*.

1 This is the computer game _____ my parents gave me for my birthday.
2 Is this the shop _____ you usually buy your lunch?
3 My uncle, _____ company designs computer games, is a very rich man.
4 Sandra is the girl _____ invited me to your party.
5 I don't understand people _____ don't enjoy sports.
6 Last year we went to California, _____ a lot of computer software is designed.
7 What's the address of the games review website _____ you were telling me about?
8 The girl _____ won the competition was only 13 years old.
9 *Minecraft* is a game _____ is really good fun to play.
10 I prefer to play games in my room, _____ I'm not likely to be disturbed.

2 Which of the sentences in Exercise 1 contain pronouns which can be replaced by *that*?

_____

3 Choose the correct relative pronouns and put the commas in the correct place.

0 My brother, (who) / *which* is two years older than me, doesn't like games.
1 I played for five hours yesterday *that* / *which* is much too long.
2 Hollywood *which* / *where* the American film industry is based is an expensive place to live.
3 John *that* / *who* lives next door to me has a huge collection of games.
4 This is my friend Stella *whose* / *that* dad works in the same office as my dad.
5 The game takes place in a city called Titania *which* / *that* is attacked by aliens.
6 The games shop in the mall *which* / *where* my cousin Max works has a sale this week.

4 Correct the mistakes in three of the sentences. Which two are correct?

1 I suggest we visit the National History Museum, wich I have never seen before. _____

2 Thanks for your letter, which I received last week. _____

3 He had a best friend, that was more like a brother to him. _____

4 I'll help to prepare the things that we need for the party. _____

5 It was nice for those attended. _____

VOCABULARY Nouns: *-ness* and *-ment*

1 Write the noun forms of the words in the correct column of the table.

	-ness	-ment
1 argue		
2 arrange		
3 dark		
4 embarrass		
5 encourage		
6 fit		
7 friendly		
8 tired		
9 treat		
10 weak		

2 Match the nouns in Exercise 1 to their meanings.

1 the feeling of being ashamed or shy _____
2 when someone or something is not strong _____
3 talk or behaviour that gives you confidence to do something _____
4 an angry discussion with someone in which you disagree _____
5 the quality of behaving in a kind, pleasant way to someone _____
6 the condition of being physically strong and healthy _____
7 the feeling when you want to rest or sleep _____
8 when there is little or no light _____
9 the use of drugs, exercises, etc. to cure a person of an illness or injury _____
10 plan for how something will happen _____

3 Complete the sentences with nouns from Exercises 1 and 2.

1 He won't do it on his own – he needs some help and _____.
2 The best _____ for flu is rest and lots of liquids.
3 Can you imagine my _____ at not knowing the answer to such an easy question!?
4 We were all made very happy by the _____ of the hotel staff – they were very kind to us.
5 The storm caused an electrical failure and the whole house was in complete _____ for hours.
6 They haven't spoken to each other since they had that terrible _____ about computer games.
7 He'll need to improve his _____ if he wants to get picked for the athletics team.
8 She had to quit the race because of _____.

1 How many films can you think of that are based on computer games?

2 Quickly read the film review. Match the highlighted phrases in the text to the adjectives in the box. Write them below.

> packed with   superb   ancient
> ridiculous   dreadful

1 ....
2 ....
3 ....
4 ....
5 ....

A
On the whole, I wouldn't recommend the *Super Mario Bros.* movie. If you are a fan of the game, you will be disappointed. It's fun to play, but not to watch!

B
Super Mario Bros. is a classic computer game which I love to play, so I decided to watch the film. The film is ¹very old (it was made in 1993), and the story is basically the same as the game – two brothers called Mario and Luigi try to rescue a princess from an evil king.

C
What I did like about the film were the special effects, which were ²very good. This is quite surprising for such an old film. The soundtrack wasn't too bad.

D
I'm sorry to say I didn't enjoy the film as much as the game. The story was ³very silly – it didn't really make any sense. It was ⁴very full of jokes that weren't funny – in fact, they were ⁵really bad. The acting wasn't much good either.

3 The review in Exercise 2 is in the wrong order. Match the paragraphs (A–D) to the headings (1–4).

1 Introduction ....
2 Negative points ....
3 Positive points ....
4 Conclusion ....

4 Is the review mostly positive, mostly negative or equally mixed? ....

5 Think of a film which is based on a game or a book you've read. Use the table below to help you plan a review of it.

Paragraph	Notes	Possible adjectives
Introduction / What it's about		
Positive points		
Negative points		
Would you recommend it?		
Conclusion		

6 Write an answer to the question in 140–190 words. Use your notes in Exercise 5.

> **You see this notice on a school website:**
>
> **Reviews wanted**
> Write a review of a film which is based on a game or a book you've read. What happens in the film? What do you like or dislike about it? Would you recommend it to other people of your age?

6 LIVE TO EAT!

Food and drink: phrasal verbs

1 Match the verbs in box A to the prepositions in box B to make phrasal verbs. Then write them next to their meanings.

A

cut	eat	eat	cool	fill
go	heat	live		

B

off	on	out	down	out
up	up	up on		

1 _____ : become full and unable to eat more
2 _____ : stop eating or drinking something
3 _____ : eat in a restaurant
4 _____ : only eat a particular type of food
5 _____ : eat all the food you have been given
6 _____ : make food hot so it can be eaten
7 _____ : stop being good to eat because it is too old
8 _____ : become less hot

2 Complete the sentences with the correct form of the phrasal verbs from Exercise 1.

1 We don't _____ much because restaurants are expensive in this town.
2 Wait for your soup to _____ a bit before you eat it, or you'll burn yourself.
3 You can't have any pudding unless you _____ everything on your plate, Charlie!
4 I don't want to cook, so I'll just _____ something in the microwave.
5 If you haven't had enough at the end of a meal, you can always _____ fruit.
6 I have _____ tea and coffee completely and I'm sleeping much better now.
7 If you don't drink that milk soon, it will _____ .
8 We more or less _____ rice and potatoes at home – it's a bit boring, to be honest.

3 Write sentences in the correct tense and add the correct prepositions.

0 Mum and Dad / eat / together / once a month
Mum and Dad eat out together once a month.
1 I / heat / some milk / for / hot chocolate / right now

2 This meat / go, / it / smell / dreadful

3 You / must / eat / all / your vegetables, Annie

4 No dessert for me, thanks. / I / already / fill / that pie

5 My sister / cut / chocolate / from her diet last month

6 Luke's brother / almost / live / meat and potatoes

READING

1 Look at the photo. What is the man's job?
_____

2 Quickly read the article on page 25. What things make Dan Hodges unusual?
_____

YOUNG CHEF

Dan Hodges has always been a bit different. At the age of eight, when all the other kids were outside playing football or in their bedrooms playing computer games, Dan was in the kitchen preparing dinner with his mum. When the other kids were watching football on TV, he was watching cooking programmes featuring his favourite chefs. Even schoolwork was just a distraction from Dan's true obsession: food.

Now, at the age of 18, the young man with film-star good looks has become one of the country's youngest head chefs. 'It really is all I've ever wanted to do,' he said. 'I'm living the dream.'

Perhaps unsurprisingly, as a baby Dan was quite a fussy eater. According to his mother, Sarah, he didn't like anything with fish or potatoes. 'He used to drive me crazy,' she told us. 'His older sister would eat anything we gave her, but Dan was much harder to please.' He used to watch, fascinated, when his mother was preparing meals and, as soon as he was able, he started to lend a hand in the kitchen. But it wasn't until he won a cooking contest at the age of 11 that his parents realised he had real talent. The prize was a one-on-one lesson at a local restaurant, where he learned how to properly prepare and cook chicken – and after that, there was no stopping him.

Kids are naturally messy, and Sarah's kitchen looked like a battlefield at times, but she didn't mind. 'Dan liked to experiment, and I gave him free range,' she said. There were, inevitably, a few accidents, but she regarded them as part of the learning process. 'I never said 'no' because I thought something was too dangerous. I'd just keep an eye on him, and only help if he needed me.'

Dan's skill and creativity continued to develop into his teen years, until his big break came when, at the age of 14, he won TV's *Young Chef* competition – and national fame arrived. 'It was weird when people started recognising me in the street,' says Dan. 'It was a bit of a shock. It used to get on my nerves when people I didn't know started talking to me. I'm used to it now. It doesn't bother me.' TV fame led on to advertising deals and eventually, his current job as head chef in one of the west of England's most exclusive restaurants. He appears to be much more comfortable when he's in the kitchen, away from the public gaze.

Does Dan have any tips for budding chefs who want to follow in his footsteps? 'Having a mum who lets you make a mess of her kitchen helps,' he laughs. Not everyone, of course, is so lucky. 'But seriously, you have to be committed. People will tell you anything is possible with hard work, but there's more to it than that. You can go to school and get top marks in all your tests – but if you don't feel it, if you don't have that passion, you should do something else, because it's not an easy life.' When he tells me he works from 7 am to midnight every day, you can see his point!

A London publisher recently offered Dan a contract to write a book, which they are confident would be a bestseller. 'I'm not sure, though. I'm not much of a writer, and I'm so busy in the restaurant, doing what
line 51 I love. It isn't really a priority for me at the moment.' Most successful chefs would jump at such a chance. Indeed, many of them have. But, as I said, Dan Hodges has always been a bit different.

3 Read the article again. For questions 1–6, choose the answer which you think fits best according to the text.

1 What is the author doing in the first paragraph?
A Showing that Dan was a rather lonely child.
B Explaining why Dan is the way he is.
C Emphasising that Dan is interested in one thing.
D Describing Dan's family background.

2 Dan's parents knew he had a talent for cooking because
A he was always very critical about food.
B he was keen to help in the kitchen.
C he had lessons from a professional.
D he came first in a competition.

3 When Dan's mother says she 'gave him free range', she means that she
A paid for all of his ingredients.
B encouraged him to cook with eggs.
C allowed him to do what he wanted.
D observed him very closely.

4 How does Dan feel about being famous?
A He gets annoyed when strangers talk to him.
B He has become accustomed to the attention.
C He is glad because it has led to a successful career.
D He is surprised that people are interested in him.

5 What advice does he give to young people who want to become chefs?
A Get the relevant qualifications first.
B Ask your parents to support you.
C Be certain it is what you want to do.
D Work as hard as you can.

6 What does 'it' refer to in line 51?
A writing a book
B being busy
C a publisher
D a restaurant

4 Underline the parts of the text which tell you the answers.

5 Match the highlighted words in the text to the definitions.

1 try something in order to discover what it's like ....
2 happening or existing now ....
3 something that is very important and must be done before other things ....
4 when you are known or recognised by many people ....
5 including someone or something as an important part ....

1 Choose the correct options to complete the sentences.

1 I *read / 've read* 12 books since the start of this year.
2 Let's go to a restaurant tonight – we *didn't eat / haven't eaten* out for weeks.
3 What *did you cook / have you cooked* for dinner last night?
4 Danielle *went / has gone* for a run and she isn't back yet.
5 I'm not hungry because I *just have / 've just had* a big lunch.
6 He still *didn't find / hasn't found* the recipe he's looking for.
7 We *often helped / have often helped* in the kitchen when we were children.
8 *Did you finish / Have you finished* your maths homework yet?

2 Write questions in the present perfect or past simple.

0 **A:** How long / you / be / a chef / ?
   How long have you been a chef?
   B: It'll be two years next month.
1 **A:** What time / you / have / lunch / ?

   B: One o'clock.
2 **A:** you / try / the new café / yet / ?

   B: No, not yet.
3 **A:** you / enjoy / the meal / ?

   B: Yes, it was great.
4 **A:** How many / cups of coffee / you / have / so far today / ?

   B: Let me think – four! That's too many!
5 **A:** Where / you / find / your mobile / ?

   B: In my bag. It was there all the time.
6 **A:** How / the weather / be / recently / ?

   B: Awful, I'm afraid.
7 **A:** you / see / this TV show / before / ?

   B: Yes, several times.
8 **A:** James / call you / yesterday evening / ?

   B: Yes, but I couldn't speak to him.

3 Complete the email with the present perfect or past simple form of the verbs in brackets.

Dear Harry,

Thank you so much for the international recipe book that you [1]＿＿＿＿＿＿＿ (give) me for my birthday last week. I [2]＿＿＿＿＿＿＿ (already / use) it three times! All the meals I [3]＿＿＿＿＿＿＿ (make) so far have been delicious.

Last night I [4]＿＿＿＿＿＿＿ (cook) a Japanese dish and tomorrow I'm going to try an Ethiopian recipe. Nobody in my family [5]＿＿＿＿＿＿＿ (ever / eat) Ethiopian food before, so they are all looking forward to it.

[6]＿＿＿＿＿＿＿ (you / try) Ethiopian food before? [7]＿＿＿＿＿＿＿ (you / enjoy) it?

See you soon!

Tina

4 Complete the conversation with the present perfect or past simple form of the verbs in brackets.

A: [1]＿＿＿＿＿＿＿ (you / see) that new burger place in the shopping mall?
B: Yes, I have.
A: How long [2]＿＿＿＿＿＿＿ (be) there?
B: I think it [3]＿＿＿＿＿＿＿ (be) open for about a month. That's right, it [4]＿＿＿＿＿＿＿ (open) just before I [5]＿＿＿＿＿＿＿ (go) on holiday last month.
A: [6]＿＿＿＿＿＿＿ (you / try) it yet?
B: Yes, I [7]＿＿＿＿＿＿＿ (eat) there last week, and Lara and I [8]＿＿＿＿＿＿＿ (spend) a few hours in there – the atmosphere's quite good, but the burger I [9]＿＿＿＿＿＿＿ (have) there [10]＿＿＿＿＿＿＿ (not be) great.
A: Oh, OK. I don't think I'll try it then!

5 Correct the mistakes in five of the sentences. Which one is correct?

1 I realise how tired you must be after the long journey you had. ＿＿＿＿＿
2 How has modern technology changed your daily life? ＿＿＿＿＿
3 I have worked on a farm in Turkey last summer. ＿＿＿＿＿
4 In my opinion, this is one of the best movies I've ever seen, and it was already nominated for several awards. ＿＿＿＿＿
5 I have been very disappointed when I read your advertisement. ＿＿＿＿＿
6 He is the greatest person I know because he is always there for his family, and he still achieved a lot in his career. ＿＿＿＿＿

1 Write the adverb forms of the adjectives.

1 accidental ....
2 basic ....
3 complete ....
4 deep ....
5 dramatic ....
6 extreme ....
7 happy ....
8 incredible ....
9 mere ....
10 necessary ....
11 physical ....
12 terrible ....
13 typical ....
14 sensible ....

2 Match adverbs in Exercise 1 to the meanings.

1 in a pleased way
2 in a way that shows all the characteristics expected from a person, thing or group ....
3 by chance or mistake ....
4 very badly ....
5 very, or much more than usually ....
6 used to introduce a short explanation about something ....
7 in every way or as much as possible ....
8 in a way that relates to the body or someone's appearance ....
9 suddenly or obviously ....
10 used in negatives to mean 'in every case' or 'therefore' ....

1 You will hear an interview with a girl who is allergic to something. What kind of things can people be allergic to?

....

2 Read the questions in Exercise 3 and underline the key words.

03 3 Listen to an interview with a teenage food blogger. For questions 1–7, choose the best answer (A, B or C).

1 Why did Davina become interested in food?
  A She was bored of eating the same things.
  B Her mother encouraged her to change her diet.
  C Nobody else in her family could cook well.

2 How does she feel when her friends question her about her diet?
  A Annoyed that they don't understand.
  B Happy to explain the situation.
  C Keen to get them to adopt more healthy diets.

3 When she goes out with friends, she
  A often comments on what they are eating.
  B sometimes eats things she shouldn't.
  C brings her own food to share.

4 How does she feel about modern British food?
  A excited by the way it is developing
  B confident that it is becoming healthier
  C happy that it is more environmentally friendly

5 What is the most important thing for Davina now?
  A keeping her blog up to date
  B getting enough rest to stay healthy
  C continuing her studies

6 Davina tells the story about her brother in a supermarket in order to show
  A how she has changed her family's attitude to food.
  B how she is very different from him.
  C how unhealthy sugary drinks are.

7 What advice does she give parents who want to improve their children's diet?
  A Introduce change gradually.
  B Get rid of unhealthy food options.
  C Show them a better way by example.

03 4 Listen to the interview again and check your answers in Exercise 3.

7 TEEN FICTION

VOCABULARY — Fiction: adjectives and nouns

1 Complete the table with the words in the box. Some words can go in both columns.

> chapter   character   complex
> illustrations   issue   major
> minor   moving   novel   opening
> plot   predictable   stunning   role

Nouns	Adjectives

2 Complete the sentences with nouns from Exercise 1.

1 The opening _____ was so bad that I didn't bother reading any further.
2 I knew he had a major _____ in the play because his name was the same size as the title on the poster.
3 They must have hired a brilliant artist because this book is worth the money for the stunning _____ alone.
4 There are no surprises in this book because it has such a predictable _____.
5 The teacher read us a very moving _____ about a child who was brought up by wolves.
6 The sensitive treatment of a very complex _____ is what makes this book so special.
7 Peter, the son of the landowner, is only a minor _____ in the book. He doesn't appear much.

3 Complete each sentence with an adjective and a noun from Exercise 1.

0 Have you read the latest thriller by J.L. Jones? It's terrible – it's got such a _predictable plot_ .
1 Success came when she was given a _____ in a Hollywood film.
2 It's unusual for a very young author to attempt to write about such a difficult and _____.
3 Most authors try to capture the reader's interest in the _____ to make sure that they continue reading.
4 Nobody thought the writing was very good, but we all agreed that the _____ in the book were very colourful and beautiful.
5 Every now and again I just have to read a _____ that makes me feel strong emotions.
6 Although Helen was only a _____ in the book, she was one of my favourites.

READING

1 How many ways can you think of to read a book?

2 Read the opening paragraph in Exercise 3 and the rest of the article on page 29. Do they mention your ways of reading from Exercise 1?

3 Use the word given in capitals at the end of some of the lines to form a word that fits in the gap in the same line. You may need to make spelling changes, and you will need to make some words plural.

Reading in the digital age

Do you read for [0]_pleasure_ or only if you have to, for school? Before the internet, children and teenagers used to read a wide [1]_____ of fiction, from comics, to novels and books of short stories. Maybe one of your older [2]_____ has told you of the times when the book they were reading was so exciting – and they were so [3]_____ to find out what happens next – that they would read it under the bedclothes at night with a torch. Of course, that was at a time when television and video 'on demand' were [4]_____. Today most of our [5]_____ is to be found online, and teens spend time on social media instead of reading books. [6]_____, their ability to concentrate is being affected and young people have a shorter attention span than their parents and grandparents. At least that's what many people believe. However, the [7]_____ is quite different. In fact, modern research [8]_____ exactly the opposite.	PLEASE VARY RELATE PATIENCE AVAILABLE ENTERTAIN CONSEQUENCE TRUE PROOF

In contrast to what a lot of older people think, teens don't in fact just use new technologies to talk to their friends. Although teenagers may not be reading books, that does not mean they are not reading. A World Book Day survey of teenage reading habits revealed over 40% read books on a computer, almost 20% on a mobile device and around 14% on a tablet, with around 10% reading on an e-reader.

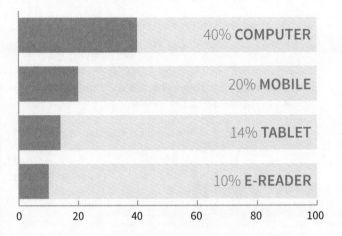

Why should this be? Well, the British telecommunications supervisor, Ofcom, points out that children as young as six understand digital technology better than adults. They are 'digital natives' – that is, they were born at a time when the internet was already part of everyday life, and take it for granted. Teens today have never known a time without the internet, so it is as natural to them to use internet-enabled devices as it was to their parents to use books.

So, what are teenagers reading? You might think that the smaller reading surface of a smartphone or tablet would make it difficult to read long books, but this is not the case. Today's teens still like to read the classics as well as modern fiction and have no difficulty in reading

them on a digital device. Adventure, crime and spy stories are all popular, with some authors such as John Grisham and Ian Rankin as popular among teens as adults. Among the classics, Charles Dickens remains a favourite, along with Jules Verne and Alexandre Dumas.

The classics do not only include novels. Cartoon characters like Tintin and Asterix are as popular today as they were in the mid-20th century. It isn't only older comic-style books that are proving popular with teens these days either – the modern-day comic, the graphic novel, is gaining in popularity everywhere. So it seems there is no danger of young people losing the habit of reading any time soon!

4 **Write questions about the article for these answers.**

0 *Why did children use to read under the bedclothes with a torch?*
Because they were impatient to find out what happened next in their book.

1 ....
That technology and social media affect concentration.

2 ....
Because they've never known a time without the internet.

3 ....
John Grisham and Ian Rankin, for example.

4 ....
The graphic novel.

5 **Match the highlighted words and phrases in the text to the definitions.**

1 tells someone about some information ....

2 pieces of writing, musical recordings, or films that are well known and of a high standard ....

3 forget how lucky you are to have something ....

4 an examination of behaviour or opinions made by asking questions ....

5 the top or outside part of something ....

1 Choose the correct answers. Sometimes two answers are correct.

1 I ____ swim until I was 15 years old.
   A couldn't   B managed to
   C wasn't able to
2 How ____ fix Mark's computer?
   A could you   B did you manage to
   C managed you to
3 Stella could read before she ____ walk.
   A was able to   B could
   C might be able to
4 Tom has hurt his leg, so we ____ play tennis next weekend.
   A won't be able to   B couldn't
   C didn't manage to
5 In the end, I ____ persuade my dad to buy me a scooter.
   A was able to   B managed to
   C will be able to
6 Tickets are going to be very difficult to get, but with luck we ____ buy some on the internet.
   A could   B might be able to
   C will be able to
7 ____ finish your project on time last week?
   A Did you manage to B Could you
   C Will you be able to
8 It was hard work, but eventually I ____ climb over the garden wall.
   A managed to   B could
   C was able to

2 Complete the sentences with the correct form of be able to and the verbs in the box.

beat	come	go	help
mend	play	see	visit

1 I'm not sure yet, but I _____ (not) to your party tomorrow.
2 When we climbed to the top of the mountain, we _____ the whole city.
3 I think I _____ this bicycle – it could be easy, or it could be impossible.
4 When I get a car, we _____ anywhere we like at the weekend!
5 I asked Olivia for advice, but she _____ (not) me.
6 Even if you train every day for a year, you _____ (not) me in a 100-metre race!
7 She hopes she _____ her grandmother soon.
8 We _____ (not) football tomorrow – it depends on the weather.

3 Correct the mistakes in five of the sentences. Which one is correct?

1 He thought he can swim.
   _____

2 He is so sly that he managed to avoid detection for a long period by pretending to be a good man.
   _____

3 It was the first time a song could make me cry.
   _____

4 As I ordered him not to move, I could call the police.
   _____

5 Even though he was born into a poor family, he managed it to go to school.
   _____

6 We decided to find a job in order to can get the money for Carla's present.
   _____

1 Match the prepositions in the box to the adjectives.

about	at	by	for	on	to	with (x2)

1 addicted ____   5 keen ____
2 annoyed ____   6 nervous ____
3 disappointed ____   7 surprised ____
4 furious ____   8 suitable ____

2 Complete each sentence with an adjective and a preposition from Exercise 1.

1 I always get _____ exams, and never sleep well the night before.
2 Our teacher gets very _____ students talking in class, and sometimes shouts at them.
3 I thought her first novel was great, but I was _____ her second one, which wasn't nearly as good.
4 Dan's _____ computer games – he just can't stop playing them.
5 My dad was absolutely _____ me when I crashed my bike into his car.
6 The organisers were _____ the number of people who turned up – they weren't expecting so many.
7 This book is quite frightening, so it isn't _____ young children.
8 I'm not really _____ novels, but I read a lot of comics.

1 Read the task. Is this going to be a happy or a sad story?

....

Send us a story!
We are looking for stories to publish on our teenage fiction website. Your story must begin with this sentence:
My best friend phoned me on my mobile, sounding very excited.
Your story must include:
- a celebrity
- an invitation

Write your **story**.

2 Make some notes for the story in Exercise 1.

1 What did your friend say?

....

2 How did you feel?

....

3 What did you do next?

....

4 What happened?

....

3 Read the story. Is it similar to your notes in Exercise 2? Does it include all the information from the task in Exercise 1?

....

My best friend phoned me on my mobile, sounding very excited. 'You won't believe this,' she said, 'but Scott Moss is at the bookshop in town. He's signing copies of his books.'
I didn't believe her at first, but she [1] .... convinced me she was telling the truth. [2] ....
I became very excited. Scott Moss is my favourite comic book artist. I've been reading his stuff for years. [3] .... was my big chance to meet him!
'I'll be there as soon as I can,' I told my friend, [4] .... I grabbed the latest Scott Moss comic book, and jumped onto my bike. It was raining but I didn't care – I was going to meet the most outstanding comic book artist in the country!
[5] .... I arrived at the bookshop, my friend came up to me. We joined the queue of people waiting to meet Scott. [6] ...., my turn came, and I told him about my ambition to be a comic book artist. I couldn't believe it when he invited me to visit him at his studio! What a day!

4 Complete the story with the words and phrases in the box.

as soon as	finally	in the end
now	that's when	then

5 Use your notes from Exercise 2 to write your own story for the task in Exercise 1.

- Use words and phrases to move the action forward.
- Write 140–190 words.
- Check your spelling and grammar.

8 GETTING AWAY

Holiday activities

1 Match the prepositions in the box to the verbs to make phrasal verbs connected to holiday activities.

around	down	out	up	up

1 chill ....   4 stay ....
2 cool ....   5 wander ....
3 sign ....

2 Choose two correct answers to complete the sentences.

1 Last holiday, I hired ...... for an afternoon.
   A a jet ski   **B** a tour   **C** a motorbike
2 We always like socialising with the ...... when we're on holiday.
   A local people   **B** wildlife   **C** other tourists
3 Did you go ...... when you were in Spain last year?
   A up all night   **B** trekking   **C** sailing
4 It's a good idea to sign up for ...... when you go to a new place.
   A an organised tour   **B** excursions
   C a tan
5 Last year we went cruising on ...... for our holiday.
   A a yacht   **B** a bus   **C** a huge ship

3 Complete the email with the words in the box.

chill	cooled	hired	photographed
signed	socialised	stayed	tan
took	wandered	went	

Hi Hunter!

We have just had a lovely holiday in Spain. We stayed on a quiet campsite near the coast where we could ¹ .... out all day if we wanted. I ² .... a jet ski on the first day, while my parents and sister sunbathed on the beach. In the evening, we ³ .... with the other campers, which was great. On the third day we ⁴ .... up all night! The day after that we were very tired, so we just ⁵ .... around the local town a bit.

Then, on the following day, we ⁶ .... up for an organised tour and ⁷ .... the sights. On the day before we left we ⁸ .... trekking in the mountains in the morning, ⁹ .... some selfies, and then, before it got too hot, we came back to the beach and ¹⁰ .... down in the sea. We all got a great ¹¹ .... to show off to our friends at home!

How was your holiday?

Lauren

4 Complete the questions with the correct form of phrasal verbs from Exercise 1. Then match them to the answers below.

1 Have you ever .... all night? ....
2 How do you .... when you're hot? ....
3 Do you like .... and seeing new things when you're on holiday? ....
4 Have you ever .... for diving classes on holiday? ....
5 What's your favourite way to .... and relax? ....

a Once, when my parents had a party!
b Yes, I love exploring different places.
c I like closing my eyes and listening to music.
d No, I don't like being underwater!
e I sit with my feet in water.

READING

1 Look at the photo on page 33. Why do you think the family is famous?

....

2 Read the text quickly. Where do you think it comes from?

A a book   **B** a magazine   **C** a travel brochure

3 Read the article again and choose the correct answers.

1 What is meant by the phrase 'putting down roots' (line 8)?
   A creating a permanent home
   B making money
2 Why did Mr and Mrs Zapp want to go on a long journey?
   A because their family was unkind to them
   B because their lives did not feel complete
3 How did the Zapps' relatives feel about their journey?
   A pessimistic
   B optimistic
4 Why do they call their children's education 'worldwide schooling' (line 31)?
   A because they learn a lot of geography
   B because they learn while they are travelling
5 What is the main advantage of travelling in a very old car?
   A It attracts a lot of attention on the road.
   B It allows them to meet new people when it breaks down.

Are we there yet?

Imagine travelling around the world with your family, by car, for 19 years straight. For some it would be like a dream come true. For others, it would get boring pretty quickly. But Argentinian couple Herman and Candelaria Zapp, along with their four children – all born on the road – are living the dream.

The couple spent their first few years of married life putting down roots in Argentina, where Herman had his own computer and telephone IT company, and they had a nice house with a swimming pool. 'Our family was happy with us. We had it all,' said Herman Zapp.

But something was missing: that around-the-world trip they had talked about, and children. So, the couple set out on a pre-baby road trip from Buenos Aires to Alaska. But they didn't get much support. 'Our family was saying that we wouldn't make it,' Zapp said. 'The most optimistic were giving us a week's journey. No more.'

Not only did the couple complete their nearly 44,000-mile initial journey, but they decided to keep going. Since then, they've been to 95 countries and travelled over 218,000 miles.

Each of their four children was born in a different country: Pampa in the United States, Tehue in Argentina, Paloma in Canada and Wallaby, the youngest, in Australia. The Zapps educate their kids themselves but also say the experiences they get are incredibly educational. 'Imagine taking your kids and watching the space shuttle take off, looking at polar bears in Alaska, seeing kangaroos in Australia and learning to speak the language of the country you're in,' Zapp said. 'We call it worldwide schooling.'

For their entire 19-year adventure, the Zapps have been travelling in a 1928 car that can't go faster than 40 miles per hour. Part tent, part kitchen, part schoolhouse and part rolling apartment, the car is definitely also a part of the family. They call it 'Grandpa'. 'I am not a mechanic at all, but every time we have a breakdown, we get a new friend,' said Zapp. 'Once we broke down in Puebla, a beautiful city in Mexico. When I looked at the engine, someone showed up right away and told me about a car museum nearby. We went there and they took apart a car on show to give us the part.' Not only did the museum not charge for that part, but the town organised a party for the Zapps, complete with a mariachi band and plenty of food.

In late 2018, the Zapps set sail from the Canary Islands back to South America on the final part of their incredible world tour.

4 What do these numbers from the article refer to?

1 19 ....

2 44,000 ....

3 40 ....

4 218,000 ....

5 Match the highlighted words and phrases in the text to the definitions.

1 when a vehicle or machine stops working for a period of time ....

2 start a journey by boat or ship ....

3 be successful ....

4 whole or complete, with nothing missing ....

5 a piece of a machine or vehicle ....

GRAMMAR — Future (1): plans and intentions

1 Cross out the adverb in *italics* which is in the wrong place.

0 We *probably* won't ~~probably~~ have time to visit all the sites in one week.

1 *Definitely* I'll *definitely* email you as soon as I arrive.

2 You *certainly* aren't *certainly* going to need any warm clothes when you visit us in Jamaica!

3 He *probably* will *probably* be back by the end of the month.

4 *Certainly* I'll *certainly* enjoy my trip to New York this summer.

5 It's *definitely* not *definitely* going to rain this afternoon.

2 Choose the correct options to complete the sentences.

1 **A:** It's cold in here.
B: OK, I *'ll / 'm going to* close the window.

2 **A:** Our train *will leave / leaves* at 4.45. We need to hurry.
B: That's OK. I *'ll drive / 'm driving* you to the station.

3 **A:** I *'ll go / 'm going to go* swimming after school. Do you want to come?
B: Sure! I *'m going / 'll go* home and get my stuff.

4 **A:** *Are you taking / Will you take* some warm clothes with you when you go camping this weekend?
B: No, Mum. I've seen the weather forecast. It *'s being / 's going to be* really hot!

3 Complete the sentences with the correct future tenses and your own ideas.

0 **A:** Can I get you something to drink?
B: Yes, please. *I'll have orange juice, please.*

1 **A:** What do you want to study at university?
B: I've made up my mind. I ....

2 **A:** Dinner will be ready at seven o'clock. Don't be late.
B: But I already have plans! I ....

3 **A:** Do you want to come camping with us this weekend?
B: Sorry, I'd love to but I can't. I ....

4 **A:** I don't feel very well. I feel dizzy.
B: Sit down. I ....

4 Correct the mistakes in four of the sentences. Which one is correct?

1 She won't definitely come to the party.
....

2 I am sure that you will enjoy yourselves very much.
....

3 Please let me know what you will do next week.
....

4 I will cook something special from my country and I am sure that you would like it!
....

5 We will discuss it when you will come home.
....

VOCABULARY — Phrasal verbs: travel

1 Complete the phrasal verbs with the correct prepositions. Then complete the definitions with a word or phrase from the box.

bill	holiday	home	~~key~~	leaving
look at	place	show	stop	

0 check ___in___ : arrive and get the ___key___ at a hotel

1 check ....: pay the ...., return your key, and leave a hotel

2 get ....: travel or move from place to ....

3 get ....: to go on ...., often because you need a rest

4 look ....: visit a place and .... the things in it

5 see ....: to go to the place where someone is .... and say goodbye

6 stop ....: .... somewhere briefly during a longer journey

7 stay ....: spend the night somewhere other than ....

8 take ....: .... someone the best parts of a certain place

2 Complete the sentences with the correct form of the phrasal verbs from Exercise 1.

1 She's been working very hard and needs to .... for a few days.

2 We .... the island on motorbikes we hired for the week.

3 Sally is .... at her best friend's house this evening.

4 It's too far to drive in one day, so we'll .... in Las Vegas for the night.

5 After I had .... at the hotel, I went up to my room and slept for five hours.

6 I'll come and .... you at the airport tomorrow.

7 An hour after I ...., I realised I'd left my mobile charger in the hotel room.

8 I've never been to this city before, so I'd like to find someone to .... me ....

9 Let's .... this place for a while before we decide whether or not to stay here.

1 Look at the photo. Where do you think it is?

2 Have you ever been on a school trip? Where did you go?

3 Read the sentences in Exercise 4. What type of words are missing: nouns, adjectives or verbs? Which sentence is missing a number? Which is missing a date?

 4 Listen to a girl called Connie talking to a group of students about a school trip to South Africa. For questions 1–10, complete the sentences with a word or short phrase.

1 The school trip to South Africa costs _____ pounds altogether.
2 It was Connie's interest in _____ which made her decide to go to South Africa.
3 Connie says she ate too much _____ when she was in South Africa.
4 Some students suffered from _____ while they were on the trip.
5 The students watched a _____ game when they were in Cape Town.
6 The students stayed with _____ when they weren't staying in a hotel.
7 Connie was surprised by the _____ she saw in Cape Town.
8 The fact that they didn't see any _____ when they were on safari disappointed Connie.
9 Connie believes her _____ has grown as a result of the trip.
10 Connie advises students to get their application forms in by _____ at the latest.

VOCABULARY Money

1 Choose the correct options to complete the sentences.

1 You'll never be financially *independent* / *short of cash* if you don't get a job.
2 We're on a very tight *debit card* / *budget* this holiday because we spent a lot on the flights.
3 How much money did you *pay off* / *take out* of the bank today?
4 A family can't *pay off* / *live on* so little each month.
5 I've finally *paid off* / *taken out* that large credit card bill from the holiday.
6 Sorry, I can't come out tonight – I'm really *wealthy* / *short of cash*.
7 I need to check my *balance* / *budget* at the bank before I buy these clothes.
8 Two burgers for the price of one – I call that a *budget* / *bargain*.
9 I needed to get some money but the *cashpoint* / *PIN* was empty.
10 Are you given a regular *allowance* / *bargain*?
11 She spent all her *savings* / *bargains* on a dream holiday to the Caribbean.

2 Match the definitions to words and phrases in Exercise 1.

1 This is the amount of money you have in your account at a particular time. ....
2 Perhaps you get this from your parents every week? ....
3 This is the amount of money you allow yourself to spend over a period of time. ....
4 This is a number that is for you only; you use it to get money or pay for things. ....
5 You have these when you keep money for a particular purpose, e.g., to buy something special. ....
6 You can often get this in a shop that is closing down, when it wants to sell everything. ....
7 Most people get this piece of plastic when they open a bank account. They can get money or pay for things with it. ....
8 This word describes someone who has plenty of money – more than they need. ....
9 This is a very useful machine that you find outside banks. ....
10 This is what you'll be if you spend more money than you earn every month! ....

READING

1 You are going to read about five young people who have become financially independent by making and selling things. Match the photos (A–E) to the products (1–5).

1 cooking videos ....
2 mobile phone apps ....
3 bow ties ....
4 board games ....
5 hair products ....

2 Read the article on page 37. Which product do you like the best?

....

Young Business People

Check out our list of young businesspeople who became successful before they could drive a car!

A Leanna Archer – *Leanna's Hair*

Leanna Archer was just nine years old when she began bottling and selling her own hair gel to friends and family. Based on her great-grandmother's secret recipe, Archer's line of all-natural hair products has expanded to include a variety of hair cleansers, conditioners and treatments. At the age of 17, she was the boss of her own company and has been recognised by prominent business publications like *Forbes* and *Success Magazine*. She even started the Leanna Archer Education Foundation to help build schools and safe learning environments for children in Haiti.

B Robert Nay – *Nay Games*

In December 2010, a new mobile game app called *Bubble Ball* was launched on the Apple App Store. In its first two weeks it received more than one million downloads, beating *Angry Birds* to become the number one free app on the App Store. This game was coded entirely by Robert Nay, a 14 year old with no previous experience of writing mobile apps. He learned everything he needed to know through research online, and produced 4,000 lines of code for his physics-based puzzle game in just a month and a half. The young entrepreneur now runs his own company, Nay Games, which has released many new levels for *Bubble Ball* and has created other mobile apps.

C Lizzie Marie Likness – *Lizzie Marie Cuisine*

Like many little girls, Lizzie Marie Likness wanted to ride horses. When she was six years old, she started selling homemade cakes and biscuits at her local market in order to pay for riding lessons. Eventually, she realised that cooking was her true passion, and with Dad lending a helping hand, she built a healthy-cooking website with instructional videos to help other kids eat better. Lizzie is now a high-school senior. She has appeared on national TV, and continues to make videos in which she demonstrates her own healthy recipes to kids and parents.

D Moziah Bridges – *Mo's Bows*

Most young boys can't stand the idea of getting dressed up, but Moziah Bridges is a rare exception. After being disappointed with the bow ties available to him on the market, Bridges learned how to sew his own with the help of his grandmother. Aged just 11, he began selling his creations on the internet, and his products were soon picked up by shops all over the country. Bridges made thousands of dollars over a very short time with his bow ties and says that he eventually plans to start a children's clothing company.

E Anshul Samar – *Elementeo*

When he was nine, Anshul Samar loved playing card games. Two years later, he began developing his own game, which he called Elementeo. Samar aimed to make chemistry fun with his board-based game, in which elements from the periodic table have their own personalities. Since the first version of Elementeo, which made one million dollars in its first year, Samar has continued to update the game. He has also created a fund to help other young entrepreneurs.

---

3 Read the article again and write A, B, C, D or E for each question.

Which young businessperson …
1 taught themselves the necessary skills alone?
2 started the business to fund another activity?
3 is involved in building schools?
4 was assisted by a parent?
5 made an educational product?
6 made their product because they didn't find what they wanted?
7 gave their product away for nothing at the beginning?
8 has had their business skills publicly praised?

4 Match the highlighted words and phrases in the text to the definitions.

1 shows and explains
2 an amount of money collected for a purpose
3 someone who starts their own business
4 increased in size
5 someone or something not included in a rule or list

1 Match the examples to the meanings.

1 This city will become more crowded in the future. ....

2 You might find that you enjoy this game more as time goes on. ....

3 I'm going to pass all my exams this year – I've studied really hard. ....

4 You'll be living in a different country this time next month. ....

5 Dan may well be late home this evening – he's got football training. ....

a a strong possibility in the future
b a possibility in the future
c a general prediction about the future
d a prediction about something in progress in the future
e a prediction based on something we already know

2 Choose the correct future tense to complete the sentences.

1 I *'ll watch* / *'ll be watching* that new show on TV at 8.15 tonight.

2 Don't tell Steven your bad news. He *won't like* / *be liking* it.

3 This time next week, you *'ll lie* / *'ll be lying* on a beach in the sunshine.

4 I don't think this new product *will sell* / *will be selling* very well.

5 Don't buy her that book. She *might* / *could* not like romances.

6 Have a taste of this sauce – you *'re going to* / *may* well like it even though it's very spicy.

3 Complete the second sentence so that it has a similar meaning to the first sentence, using the word given. Sometimes more than one answer is possible.

1 Perhaps we'll meet up later. **MIGHT**
We .... later.

2 I think it's very possible that Danny will forget to invite somebody. **WELL**
Danny .... to invite somebody.

3 You might become quite rich because of your business idea. **MAKE**
Your business idea .... quite rich.

4 Attending university is not something she wants to do. **GOING**
She .... to university.

5 At this time, she'll still be awake. **SLEEPING**
She .... at this time.

6 I don't think we'll have enough money for a holiday this year. **MAY**
We .... enough money for a holiday this year.

4 Correct the mistakes in four of the sentences. Which one is correct?

1 After that, you will be going to have lunch. _____

2 We should use the bicycles for travelling around, because we will be having more fun. _____

3 I will be waiting for you next week. _____

4 September is not suitable for me because I will take examinations. _____

5 I'd like to go on holiday in the summer because I will study in September. _____

1 Complete the sentences with *a* or *the*.

1 There have been .... number of complaints.

2 They were delighted with .... number of cakes she sold at the fair.

3 .... number of people are joining the club.

4 I couldn't believe .... number of students who failed the test.

2 Match the adjectives to their meanings.

1 considerable ....
2 growing/ increasing ....
3 limited ....
4 maximum
5 minimum ....
6 record ....
7 reduced ....
8 unlimited ....

a describing the largest amount allowed or possible
b made less in number
c kept within a particular size, range, time, etc.
d getting bigger in size or quantity
e large or important enough to be noticed
f describing the biggest, best, highest, etc.
g describing the smallest amount allowed or possible
h without any maximum number

3 Complete the second sentence so that it has a similar meaning to the first sentence. Use an adjective from Exercise 2 and *number*.

1 The number of students is getting bigger.
There is a .... of students.

2 The number of tickets available is not as big as it was.
A .... of tickets is now available.

3 You have to buy at least two bottles to get a discount.
A .... of two bottles have to be bought to get a discount.

4 Quite a lot of people bought my app.
My app was bought by a .... of people.

5 Nobody is allowed to buy more than two tickets.
Two is the .... of tickets anyone is allowed to buy.

1 Read the task. Then read the article below it. Is the style of the article formal or informal?

You see this advert in an online teenage magazine.

> **Tell us about your IDEAL JOB**
> Everyone has to make a living somehow. Tell us how *you* would like to do it.
> • What would be your ideal job?
> • What things make this the perfect job for you?
> • Is there anything you wouldn't like about it?
> • How easy will it be for you to get this job in the future?
> **We'll publish the best articles on our website next month!**

My ideal job

A What is my ideal job? As far as I'm concerned, it would mean doing something I love doing, and getting paid well for it. I think that's the same for most people, although not many people achieve this goal. In fact I don't know anybody who has their ideal job!

B For me, the ideal job would be to work as a restaurant critic. Why? For a start, I love eating food! I also enjoy writing – so a job which combines these two things would be perfect for me. What's more, I think restaurant critics are quite well paid.

C On the other hand, I might get bored of eating out in restaurants all the time and being away from home. On top of that, there's no guarantee that the restaurant I'm reviewing will be any good. It could be terrible!

D All in all, I think I'd love to be a restaurant critic, even though I don't think there's much chance of me becoming one. There just aren't that many restaurant critics, so competition for the job would be very high.

2 Does the article answer all the questions in the task in Exercise 1?

3 Match the paragraphs A–D in the article to 1–4.
1 the bad points ....
2 the conclusion ....
3 the good points ....
4 the introduction ....

4 Look at the highlighted phrases in the article. Answer the questions.

Which …
1 emphasises what is really true?
2 introduces a personal opinion?
3 gives the first of several reasons?
4 are used to add similar ideas?

5 is used to sum up?
6 means 'although'?
7 is used to introduce a contrasting opinion?

5 Read the task in Exercise 1 again and plan your own article using the same structure as in the example article.

6 Write your article in 140–190 words. Use informal language and the phrases from Exercise 4.

10 GIVE ME A HAND

Household tasks

1 Match the verbs in the box to the nouns.

clear up	fix	fold	load	put away
sort	sweep	wash up	water	wipe

1 _____ the clothes / the towels / the paper

2 _____ the floor / the garden path / the streets

3 _____ the rubbish / the recycling / your books

4 _____ a room / a mess / a problem

5 _____ the table / the chairs / the kitchen surfaces

6 _____ your clothes / the dinner things / the shopping

7 _____ the plants / the garden / the flowers

8 _____ the dishwasher / the washing machine / the car

9 _____ the TV / the leak / the computer

10 _____ the pans / the plates / the dishes

2 Choose the correct options to complete the sentences.

1 I haven't *watered* / *sorted* the plants for weeks.

2 Will you *sweep* / *fold* your clothes and *put them away* / *clear them up* before you go to bed, please?

3 Before we can watch TV, we have to *wipe* / *sweep* the table and *put away* / *load* the dishwasher.

4 I hope you *clear up* / *sort* this mess you're making after you've finished *loading* / *fixing* your skateboard.

5 The floor is dirty – you'd better *water* / *sweep* it.

6 I've done the washing – can you *sort* / *load* it into separate piles of your clothes and your sister's clothes?

7 Don't *load* / *wipe* the dishwasher this morning because the repairman is coming to *water* / *fix* it.

8 All these plates and dishes are clean. Let's *wash them up* / *put them away*.

9 Someone has put all of the rubbish in the same bin. Now I have to go through the bin and *clear it up* / *sort it* into recycling and ordinary rubbish.

10 Meral, can you *sweep* / *wipe* the path outside the front door before your grandparents come? The trees have dropped leaves all over it.

3 Choose the odd one out in each list of verbs.

0 You can do this to your clothes.
put away   (water)   fold

1 You can do this to a room.
sweep   clear up   load

2 You can do this to a dishwasher.
water   fix   load

3 You can do this with a table.
clear up   wipe   sweep

4 You can do this with pans.
put away   fold   wash up

5 You can do this with toys.
load   sort   put away

6 You can do this with the floor.
sweep   wipe   load

7 You can do this with your bike.
fix   sweep   put away

1 Quickly read the text on page 41. Where do you think it was published?

A in a technical manual

B on a technology website

C in a science school book

2 Read the first part of the article on page 41 again. Decide which answer (A, B, C or D) best fits each gap (1–8).

	A		B		C		D
0	(A) limited	B	little	C	minor	D	narrow
1	A frequent	B	common	C	general	D	normal
2	A mixture	B	type	C	quality	D	variety
3	A missing	B	leaving	C	avoiding	D	skipping
4	A way	B	road	C	direction	D	track
5	A let	B	admit	C	allow	D	make
6	A take	B	set	C	pick	D	get
7	A travel	B	progress	C	transport	D	movement
8	A suspicious	B	doubtful	C	wrong	D	unsure

3 Read the second part of the article again more carefully and match the paragraph titles to the paragraphs D–H.

1 Kitchen robots _____

2 'Telepresence' (remote) robots _____

3 Social robots _____

4 Robot alarm clock _____

5 Toy robots _____

DOMESTIC ROBOTS

A domestic robot, or service robot, is a robot that is used for jobs around the house. There are only a ⁰ *limited* number of models around at the moment, though some people have suggested that they could become more ¹ _____ in the future. We found a wide ² _____ of them on the web.

A FLOOR CLEANING ROBOTS

These are the most popular type of domestic robots currently available. They move quickly around hard-surface flooring and carpets removing dirt and pet hair – ³ _____ obstacles like furniture and toys, and automatically finding their ⁴ _____ around.

B GRASS CUTTING ROBOTS

These sophisticated machines ⁵ _____ you to sit back in your garden and watch them do all the work! You just ⁶ _____ up a wire line around the area you want to cut, and switch it on.

C SECURITY ROBOTS

These have night-vision cameras that can detect ⁷ _____. You can programme them to move around inside or outside your house – and if anything ⁸ _____ happens, they will automatically video it and send you a text or email to tell you.

D Our favourite example of this type of robot is called UNO. It dances, plays football with you, shoots table tennis balls, sings songs – and it can recognise your voice, so that it obeys only your orders. It looks really cute too! You can also get electronic pets for the younger members of the family.

E These are similar to toy robots, but with a more serious purpose. A lot of them are designed to help older people by providing company and sometimes helping with the household tasks. In the future, we expect to see robots that are able to understand language, have conversations with you, and understand human emotions, so that they know what to do.

F A step up from social robots, these can allow you to visit a distant location and explore it as if you were there. They let healthcare workers check on patients, for example. Also, children who cannot leave their homes because they are ill or disabled can attend school using one of these!

G You need a highly-specialised robot if you want it to do the cooking for you. The one we saw was developed by a German university. It can cook pancakes and sausages, and even make sandwiches. We're not so sure about this one – you might want to supervise if it's using the cooker! You don't want the house to burn down!

H Our favourite of the bunch, this one is for people who can't get out of bed in the morning. It can be set to let you sleep a bit longer, but after that – when your extra time is up – it will scream loudly. If that doesn't work, it will jump off the bedside table and roll around the room flashing its lights and making a noise until you finally get up!

---

4 Which robot A–H would you recommend for these people?

1 'I spend a lot of time away from home, and the house is often empty.' _____
2 'It's my nephew's birthday next month. He's 12 years old.' _____
3 'I'm often late for school in the morning.' _____
4 'My grandma lives a long way from us and often gets lonely. She could also use some help around the house.' _____
5 'I hate making my own meals.' _____

5 Match the highlighted words and phrases in the text to the definitions.

1 designed to be good at a particular thing _____
2 pleasant and attractive _____
3 when you are with a person or people _____
4 watch to make sure everything is done correctly _____
5 far away _____

1 Complete the sentences with the correct passive form of the verbs in brackets.

1 Millions of domestic robots _____ (make) since the beginning of the century.
2 New technologies which can help with household tasks _____ (develop) at the moment.
3 Robots _____ (not use) for household chores in the 1970s.
4 The first successful robots _____ (create) in Japan in the 1980s.
5 Some people think that great chefs _____ (can't / replace) by robots, because good cooking is too complicated.
6 Most of the housework in this house _____ (do) by me!
7 This laboratory is totally modern and all of the experiments now _____ (conduct) by robots.
8 Robots that clean swimming pools _____ (introduce) into both of the pools in our town recently. They really keep the pools clean!

2 Complete the second sentence so that it has a similar meaning to the first sentence, using the word given. Do not change the word given. You must use between two and five words, including the word given.

0 Somebody told me these computers were cheap!
   WAS
   I _was told that_ these computers were cheap.

1 Parents shouldn't give household tasks to children under ten years old.
   GIVEN
   Children under ten years old _____ household tasks.

2 They won't allow you to go out if you don't eat your dinner.
   ALLOWED
   If you don't eat your dinner, you _____ go out.

3 Someone needs to sweep this floor.
   SWEPT
   This floor _____ by someone.

4 Nobody has cleared up this room for days.
   NOT
   This room _____ for days.

5 They are not telling us the truth.
   BEING
   We _____ the truth.

6 You must deliver this note to the headteacher this afternoon.
   BE
   This note _____ to the headteacher this afternoon.

3 Seven of the nine <u>underlined</u> clauses in the text would be better in the passive. Choose which seven and rewrite them in the passive, using *by* if you think it is necessary. The first one has been done for you.

<u>Somebody has broken into our school!</u> <u>It happened last night</u>. It was a very dark night, but <u>a person who lives nearby saw two men</u> climbing over the gate at about 11 pm. <u>Somebody else called the police.</u> <u>They arrived at 11.15</u>, but <u>they didn't find anybody in the school</u>. It seems that the burglars were very quick. <u>They stole some computers.</u> <u>The police have already arrested two men.</u> <u>The police are questioning them at the moment</u>. I hope it is them!

0 *Our school has been broken into!*
1 _____
2 _____
3 _____
4 _____
5 _____
6 _____

4 Tick (✓) the correct sentences.

1 A In the advertisement it is said that the cost of two nights is cheaper.
  B In the advertisement it says that the cost of two nights is cheaper.

2 A At last, the concert was started.
  B At last, the concert started.

3 A I would like to know if the offer includes weekends or if the cost could be raised at that time.
  B I would like to know if the offer includes weekends or if the cost could be raise at that time.

4 A We went to the football game, which was held on Saturday.
  B We went to the football game which held on Saturday.

5 A We would like to ask if some modifications could be make to the schedule.
  B We would like to ask if some modifications could be made to the schedule.

1 Complete the sentences with the correct form of *make*, *let* or *be allowed to*.

1 My parents _____ my little brother brush his teeth before he goes to bed.
2 _____ you sometimes _____ eat your dinner in front of the TV?
3 Why don't you _____ her go out? She's done all her homework!
4 He _____ stay out after 10.00 pm until he was 14 years old.
5 I don't want to go on the school trip. Please don't _____ me go!
6 Sophia's parents _____ her buy whatever clothes she likes.

2 Complete the second sentence so that it has a similar meaning to the first sentence. Use *be allowed to*, *let* or *make*.

1 Our teacher lets us eat lunch in the classroom.
We _____ in the classroom.
2 I was forced by the headmaster to stay behind after school.
The headmaster _____ after school.
3 Dan isn't allowed to ride his bike in the street.
Dan's parents _____ his bike in the street.
4 Why don't you let Carmen go to the party?
Why _____ to the party?
5 We can stay here for another half an hour.
They _____ for another half an hour.
6 I don't want to go to piano lessons, but my parents insist that I do.
My parents _____ to piano lessons, even though I don't want to.

1 Look at the photo at the bottom of the page. What do you think the relationship is between the two people?

_____

2 Have you, or anyone you know, done any voluntary work? What kind of work was it?

_____

3 You will hear a student called Simon talking about volunteering to help an elderly man called Barry for a charity organisation. For questions 1–10, complete the sentences with a word or short phrase.

1 It was Simon's interest in _____ that made him want to volunteer with Elderly Friends.
2 It took _____ for Elderly Friends to respond to Simon's application.
3 Barry said that Simon reminded him of his _____ who lived abroad.
4 Simon found it difficult to clean Barry's house because the _____ was really old.
5 Simon says that showing Barry how to use his _____ took quite a long time.
6 One of the things Simon learned from Barry was how to play _____ .
7 Simon always made _____ when he cooked for Barry.
8 Barry especially liked going to _____ with Simon.
9 Next year, Simon hopes to take his _____ so that he can go to other places with Barry.
10 Simon believes that being a _____ is the most important requirement for this kind of volunteering.

11 THE DIGITAL AGE

VOCABULARY — Technological advances

1 Match 1–9 to a–i to make compound nouns and write them below.

1	driverless	a	charger
2	fitness	b	whiteboard
3	interactive	c	tracker
4	portable	d	console
5	smart	e	watch
6	video game	f	headphones
7	virtual-reality	g	headset
8	wireless	h	car
9	smart	i	speaker

1 _____
2 _____
3 _____
4 _____
5 _____
6 _____
7 _____
8 _____
9 _____

2 Complete the sentences with the words and phrases in the box.

> driverless cars   drones   fitness tracker
> interactive whiteboard   portable charger
> smartwatch   video game console
> virtual-reality headset   wireless headphones

1 When you put on a _____, it is like entering a whole new world.
2 With a _____ you can record how far you walk every day, your heart-rate, and your calorie consumption.
3 A(n) _____ is a very useful tool for teachers to use in the classroom.
4 With a _____ you can keep your phone powered up even when you can't get to an electric power source.
5 _____ are operated by computers, and could improve road safety in the future.
6 You can send texts, make phone calls, browse the internet and, of course, tell the time with a _____.
7 Many people play for hours on a _____ and never get any work done!
8 I find _____ very useful because I can walk around the house while listening to music.
9 In the future, we'll use _____ to deliver everything from pizzas to new shoes because they can fly directly to the customer's house. It'll be much faster.

READING

1 Look at the pictures. Do you know what they are or what they represent? Label the pictures.

A _____

B _____   C _____

D _____

2 Quickly read the article on page 45 and match the people to the pictures in Exercise 1.

3 Read the article again. Complete the sentences with *DE* (Doug Engelbart), *B&L* (Babbage and Lovelace), *MZ* (Mark Zuckerberg) or *SJ* (Steve Jobs).

1 _____ and _____ failed to complete higher education.
2 _____ did not see his/her/their invention completed in his/her/their lifetime.
3 _____ started his/her/their career while still a child/children.
4 _____ got involved in the entertainment industry.
5 _____ and _____ created something which many people bought.
6 _____ and _____ had a connection with Apple computers.

GIANTS OF TECHNOLOGY

1 DOUG ENGELBART (picture ____)

In an era when computers were as big as the rooms that held them, Doug Engelbart's ideas were very advanced. He invented a lot of things, but without a doubt his most famous invention was the computer mouse.

The son of a radio repairman, Engelbart studied electrical engineering at university, and eventually became a computer researcher.

The first mouse was a wooden shell with two metal wheels, and was demonstrated in San Francisco in 1968. It was called a mouse because the tail came out of the end.

Although over a billion computer mice have been sold, Engelbart never made much money from them. His company sold Steve Jobs' Apple Computer, Inc. a licence for the technology for only about $40,000 in 1983.

2 BABBAGE AND LOVELACE (picture ____)

Charles Babbage was an English mathematician and Cambridge University graduate who had the idea of using a machine to solve maths problems. Until that time, human beings did maths on paper – and often made mistakes. In the 1830s Babbage developed what he called the Difference Engine, which was the first ever digital computer. It was the size of a small car.

Babbage's computer was programmed by Ada Lovelace, the daughter of a famous poet. She used small cards with holes in them to give instructions to the machine, and is considered by many people to be the world's first computer programmer.

Together they designed a more advanced machine called the Analytical Engine, but it wasn't actually built until 1991, when British scientists created one from Babbage's notes.

3 MARK ZUCKERBERG (picture ____)

Some kids are passionate about playing computer games. From early on in his childhood, Mark Zuckerberg loved designing them. His parents gave him a lot of encouragement for his interest in computers, and by the time he started university, he already had a reputation as a highly-skillful programmer.

In 2004, while still a student, he spent most of his time on the creation of a free website which he called 'TheFacebook'. It allowed students at his university to keep each other up to date with what they were doing in their daily lives. In the summer of that year, it grew quickly in popularity, and soon expanded to include most universities in the United States. In 2006, by that time called simply Facebook, it was launched globally for anyone over the age of 13 to use.

Today, Facebook has over two billion users worldwide and many millions more use the company's other social media apps Instagram, WhatsApp and Messenger. Mark Zuckerberg is one of the wealthiest people in the world – even though he left university in his second year.

4 STEVE JOBS (picture ____)

Probably the closest thing the computer industry has ever had to a rock star, Steve Jobs achieved success early in life after giving up university before finishing his first year. Steve Jobs and his friend Steve Wozniak then formed Apple Computer, Inc., when Jobs was just 21.

They went on to make the world's best-selling computer, called Apple II, then another called the Macintosh. Known as the Mac, it was the first personal computer to use a mouse and a graphical interface – like nearly all computers have today.

In the 1990s and 2000s, Jobs was the creative force behind such best-selling gadgets as the iPod, the iPhone and the iPad – as well as helping create award-winning animated films with Pixar Studios.

---

4 Read the text again. Are the sentences *T* (True) or *F* (False)?

1 Doug Engelbart made very large computers.
2 Engelbart's father was also involved in technology.
3 Babbage made the Difference Engine with the help of his daughter.
4 A model of the Analytical Engine was never built.
5 Mark Zuckerberg used to charge money to let people use Facebook.
6 Zuckerberg's social network site has had more than one name.
7 Steve Jobs started his business while at university.
8 Other companies copied Apple Computer, Inc.'s early products.

5 Match the highlighted words in the text to the definitions.

1 all over the world
2 started an organisation or business
3 a period of time in history
4 good at doing something
5 believed

1 Write sentences in the present perfect continuous.

1 You / play / that game / for hours / !

2 Sam and Sara / amuse / themselves / all day

3 We need to find out what / cause / the computer to crash

4 How long / you / learn / Spanish / ?

5 she / cry / for long / ?

6 No, I / not / use / your laptop

2 Choose the correct options to complete the sentences.

1 I've *thought* / *been thinking* – we should get a new computer.
2 She's never *used* / *been using* an iPad before.
3 This is the first time they've *visited* / *been visiting* London.
4 The sun has *shone* / *been shining* all day today.
5 Have you *waited* / *been waiting* here for long?
6 Sorry, I haven't *finished* / *been finishing* my homework yet.
7 You look exhausted. What have you *done* / *been doing*?
8 How long have they *known* / *been knowing* each other?

3 Complete the conversation with the present perfect continuous form of the verbs in brackets.

A: What's that you're wearing?
B: This? It's a fitness tracker – it measures the distance I run. It's really useful.
A: Oh. ¹＿＿＿＿＿ (you / use) it for long?
B: Yes, since I started running. I ²＿＿＿＿＿ (run) every day for two years now.
A: To keep fit?
B: Yes, but I enjoy it. I ³＿＿＿＿＿ (train) for a half-marathon recently.
A: Wow! How long do you run every day?
B: Well, today I ⁴＿＿＿＿＿ (jog) for about an hour, but I'm going to stop now.
A: Oh, good. I ⁵＿＿＿＿＿ (intend) to ask you about my party next weekend. Can we discuss it now?

4 Complete the email with the present perfect simple or present perfect continuous form of the verbs in brackets.

Hi Mary,

How are you? I ¹＿＿＿＿＿ (not hear) from you for ages. What ²＿＿＿＿＿ (you / do)? I ³＿＿＿＿＿ (just have) some great news! I ⁴＿＿＿＿＿ (be) accepted at the university in my home town to study computing. You know I ⁵＿＿＿＿＿ (program) computers since I was 12 years old and I ⁶＿＿＿＿＿ (want) to build a career in software design for ages – well now it's time to start studying seriously!

The trouble is, I'm so excited that I ⁷＿＿＿＿＿ (not sleep) very well since I heard. I'm working in a café at the moment, and I ⁸＿＿＿＿＿ (arrive) late a couple of times already. My boss ⁹＿＿＿＿＿ (already warn) me twice, and if I'm late again, I'll lose my job. I don't care too much, though – I ¹⁰＿＿＿＿＿ (save) quite a lot of money already.

I have to go now. Dad ¹¹＿＿＿＿＿ (ask) me all week to set up his new printer in his office, so that's what I'm going to do now. Then I'm going for a bike ride. It looks like it ¹²＿＿＿＿＿ (rain), because the roads are wet – but the sun's shining now.

Write soon!

Jackie

5 Correct the mistakes in three of the sentences. Which two are correct?

1 I study English for two years.

2 I have been playing football since I was a child, and I like it very much.

3 I like children and I have been working in a similar job before.

4 I haven't written for so long, but I have been studying for my exams.

5 I was thinking about the ideas you suggested, but I haven't decided yet.

VOCABULARY — Adjective suffixes

1 Make the adjective form of the nouns and verbs in the box and write them below with the correct suffix. Some words can go with more than one suffix.

adventure ~~afford~~ care create danger end enjoy environment fame fault impress innovate interact mystery origin profit rely season spice thought tradition use

1 -able   *affordable,* _____ (3)
2 -al   _____ (4)
3 -ful   _____ (3)
4 -ive   _____ (4)
5 -less   _____ (5)
6 -ous   _____ (4)
7 -y   _____ (2)

2 Match adjectives in Exercise 1 to the definitions.

1 willing to try new and often difficult or dangerous things
2 not giving enough attention to what you're doing
3 cheap enough to be bought by most people
4 kind and always considering how you can help other people
5 special or interesting because of not being the same as others
6 able to be trusted or believed
7 following customs or ways that have continued in a group of people for a long time
8 strange or unknown, and not explained or understood

3 Complete the sentences with adjectives in Exercise 1.

1 Thank you, we have had a very _____ evening – really great fun!
2 The latest computer game is really _____ – you can play with anyone on the internet.
3 Dan is always drawing and writing stories, because he's very _____.
4 I took my fitness tracker back to the shop because it was _____. It kept turning itself off.
5 That film seemed _____ – it was so long!
6 Do you like _____ food, like Indian food?

WRITING — A persuasive email

1 Look at the task below. Should your email be formal or informal?

> The head of your school, Mrs Amis, is planning to close down the school's wireless network. Before she does this, she is inviting students to give their opinions. Write an email to Mrs Amis. What do you think of the idea? Why do you think that way?

2 Complete the email with the words and phrases in the box.

Furthermore   In conclusion   Firstly
Nevertheless   Thank you

Dear Mrs Amis,

¹ _____ for inviting students to give our opinions about closing down the wireless network. I truly appreciate the opportunity to comment on this.
² _____, I would like to say that your reasons for wanting to close the network are understandable. Most people would agree that some students spend too much time on the internet. ³ _____, a few also use social media to bully other students, and this is completely unacceptable.
⁴ _____, I firmly believe that the students who use the network for these purposes are in a tiny minority. Why should the majority of students who use the network responsibly be punished for the actions of a few? It seems to me that closing down the network is totally unfair. What is more, access to the internet is absolutely essential to us. We need it to do research!
⁵ _____, I can say without a doubt that nearly all students at this school are strongly against closing down the wireless network. I sincerely hope that you will listen to us, and keep it open.

Regards,

Tanya Harris

3 What is the intention of the writer in the second paragraph?

4 Read the email again.

a Underline the five expressions which introduce the writer's opinion.
b Circle six adverbs which make verbs or adjectives stronger.

5 Read the task below and write your email in 140–190 words. Use the language in Exercise 4.

> The head of your school, Mr Grayling, is planning to stop allowing students to bring mobile phones in to school. Before he does this, he is inviting students to give their opinions. Write an email to Mr Grayling. What do you think of the idea? Why do you think that way?

12 MY CIRCLE OF FRIENDS

1 Use the definitions below to complete the word puzzle. Then write the mystery word in grey.

1 easily annoyed by someone's mistakes or because you have to wait
2 not liking to spend money, especially on other people
3 usually relaxed and calm, not worried or upset
4 always believing that good things will happen
5 not able to be trusted or depended on
6 a person who becomes angry and annoyed easily
7 able to be trusted or depended on
8 not noticing or not caring about other people's feelings
9 kind and always thinking about how you can help other people
10 being able to stay calm and not get angry, especially when something takes a long time

Word ↓ = _____

2 Choose the correct words to complete the sentences.

1 I know I keep making mistakes. Thanks for being so *pessimistic / patient* with me.
2 What's Annie shouting about now? She seems to be so *generous / bad-tempered* these days.
3 He's only 14, but he seems older because he's very *reliable / insensitive* for his age.
4 Sally will share her lunch with you if you forget yours; she's really *generous / unreliable*.
5 Stop messing around in class – it's so *insensitive / thoughtful* to others.
6 If you can't see the problems here, I think you're too *optimistic / bad-tempered*.

3 Complete the sentences with the __opposites__ of the adjectives in the box.

| bad-tempered | generous | insensitive |
| patient | pessimistic | reliable |

1 You should try to be more _____, because you accidentally hurt people's feelings too often.
2 I wouldn't trust Mark to be part of our team – he's totally _____.
3 Don't be so _____! Dinner will be ready in 20 minutes.
4 Danielle is really _____ – nothing seems to upset her or make her angry.
5 I'm quite _____ about the weather next weekend. The forecast isn't bad.
6 It was very _____ of you not to give your sister a present for her birthday.

READING

1 Quickly read the article on page 49 and choose the best title.

a Friendship and evolution
b Friends are good for you
c The science of friendship

2 Read the article again. Choose the answer (A, B, C or D) which you think fits best according to the article.

1 In the opening paragraph, the author shows his
   A trust in the findings of modern research.
   B concern about the consequences of loneliness.
   C suspicion that scientists might not always be correct.
   D interest in the relationship between friendship and health.

2 What does 'it' refer to in line 13?
   A the desire to be healthy
   B the necessity of relationships
   C the negative impact of evolution
   D the connection between stress and ill-health

3 When the author says 'humble acquaintance' in line 28, he/she means someone who
   A you see every day.
   B you don't know very well.
   C you meet through another friend.
   D you don't really want to be friends with.

Do you have a large circle of friends? Well, lucky you! Believe it or not, many scientists now believe that people with lots of friends live 22% longer than those with hardly any friends. It's even been suggested that having lots of friends may make it less likely that you will catch a cold. I must say, I'm not so sure about that – doesn't spending a lot of time with other people mean it's more likely you'll get more colds?

It seems that having a supportive social network can result in less stress and therefore better health. Why should this be? Well, the fact is we're sociable animals. We have evolved to live in groups, and need others
line 13 for our survival. It is genetic. So people with lots of social connections are more relaxed, easy-going, and have higher self-esteem – all of which are related to better health.

Although friends help us cope with stress, they can also cause it. Think about it – how do you feel when your best friend says something hurtful to you? People we really like can wound us more deeply than anyone when they make an insensitive comment, or let us down – because they mean so much more to us. So would we be healthier if we didn't have any friends at all? Definitely not. When it comes to circles of friends, bigger is better.

So what should you do if your social life isn't going as well as you want it to? The research here is helpful. For a start, don't underestimate the value of the
line 28 humble acquaintance. Interacting with people you see often but don't count as friends – your local shopkeeper, or that person you say 'good morning' to at the bus stop every day – can have a positive impact on your well-being. The first step is to tell them something about yourself. But if you want to build deeper friendships, you need to give it more time. Studies have found that it takes about 50 hours of socializing to become 'casual friends' with someone, 90 hours to become what would be considered 'real friends', and a total of 200 hours to become 'close friends'.

And what makes close friends so close? The old saying 'opposites attract' couldn't be further from the truth. Researchers have known for a long time that people choose friends who are the same as them in lots of ways – age, education level, politics. In fact, recent brain research has found that close friends have almost identical brain patterns!

Generally speaking, females are better at friendships than males. In stressful situations girls (and women) protect and care for others, and look for others to support them. They listen to their female friends' problems and help come up with solutions. Boys (and men) tend not to do that, as male friendships are often more about helping out with practical problems, mending things and so on. Their friendships have less emotional content.

Whatever you think about the scientific research into friendship, it is an unfortunate truth that people don't have as many friends as they used to. Or perhaps that's as many real friends. People, especially young people, have a lot of online friends these days, but the number of people who feel they have someone they can talk to about important subjects has dropped a lot: by nearly one third in the last ten years. There could be many reasons for this sad decline, but to my mind, the most likely is the growth of the internet – both the time we all spend alone with our computers, tablets and phones, and the mistaken belief that we are satisfying our social nature with virtual friendships.

4 What is most likely to produce a close friendship between two people?
   A a combination of opposing personality types
   B a willingness to share personal details
   C a large amount of time spent together
   D a similarity of many characteristics

5 Women's friendships are different from men's because women are
   A not interested in practical things.
   B more concerned with feelings.
   C more helpful in general.
   D better at fixing things.

6 What is the author's main point in the final paragraph?
   A Communication is much easier these days.
   B Technology is harmful to relationships.
   C Scientists are too optimistic.
   D True friendship is very rare.

3 Match the highlighted words in the text to the definitions.

   1 when someone or something continues to live or exist ....
   2 be (not) likely to do a particular thing ....
   3 hurt or injure someone ....
   4 when something becomes less in amount or importance ....
   5 the effect that a person or situation has on something ....

GRAMMAR   Zero and first conditionals

1 Complete the sentences with the verb in brackets. Use *will*, the imperative or the present tense.

1 If you and your friends eat all that cake, you _____ (feel) ill.
2 If you leave ice cream in the sun, it _____ (melt).
3 If you want to come to the party, _____ (call) Miranda.
4 Pasta _____ (be) disgusting if it is cooked for too long.
5 If you don't talk to Mushtaq, he _____ (not know) how you feel.
6 We _____ (go) to the swimming pool if it's sunny tomorrow.
7 You _____ (be) more likely to be ill if you have no friends.
8 If you want to sleep well, _____ (not use) a computer just before going to bed.

2 Write sentences using the zero and first conditional.

1 you / lend / me your bicycle, / I / give / it back this afternoon
2 Sara / eat / peanuts, / she / get / really ill
3 Nobody / be / your friend / you / be / mean and insensitive
4 not go / to school / you / feel / ill
5 I / might / be happier / we / move / to the countryside.
6 We / get / sunburn / we / lie / in the sun for much longer

3 Complete the sentences using the zero or first conditional. Use your own ideas.

1 If I eat too much fruit, _____
2 I'll be very happy _____
3 If I want to relax, _____
4 Our teacher gets annoyed _____

4 Correct the mistakes in three of the sentences. Which two are correct?

1 If we stay in the Swan Hotel, we eat there.
2 Drop me a line if you can!
3 I am a student, so I am to earn money, it will be better to work.
4 So in the future, using the car will be quite expensive if you drive in one of those towns.
5 If you want to visit the sights, you will go to the 'White Tower.'

VOCABULARY   Adjective and noun suffixes

1 Write the noun or adjective.

1 _____ / different
2 fitness / _____
3 _____ / generous
4 _____ / happy
5 importance / _____
6 _____ / intelligent
7 _____ / organised
8 patience / _____
9 qualification / _____
10 _____ / strong

2 Find and correct the mistakes with adjectives and nouns in five more of the sentences.

0 It takes a lot of ~~strong~~ to be able to lift your own body weight.   *strength*
1 Making good friends is one of the most importance things you will ever do.   _____
2 I'm not very patient – I can't stand waiting long for anything.   _____
3 She doesn't want to be involved in the organised of the party, but she wants to be invited.   _____
4 I think generosity is something I look for in a friend's character.   _____
5 If you want to get fitness, try exercising every day.   _____
6 There's not much different between cabbage and spinach.   _____
7 Dolphins have much more intelligent than sharks.   _____

1 What qualities does a good friend have? Make a list of three or four ideas.

....

....

....

....

2 Listen to five people talking about their best friends. Do they mention any of the qualities in your list in Exercise 1? ....

3 Listen again and complete the table with the positive and negative adjectives used to describe the friends.

	Positive adjectives	Negative adjectives
Speaker 1		
Speaker 2		
Speaker 3		
Speaker 4		
Speaker 5		

4 Listen again and choose from the list (A–H) what each speaker says about their best friend. There are three extra letters which you do not need to use.

My best friend …
A once helped me in a difficult situation.
B sometimes has an attitude which annoys me.
C can find humour in any situation.
D is often judged unfairly by people.
E has a talent which made him/her popular.
F gets anxious very easily.
G didn't use to be fond of me.
H is frequently mean to other people.

Speaker 1 ....
Speaker 2 ....
Speaker 3 ....
Speaker 4 ....
Speaker 5 ....

VOCABULARY Reporting nouns

1 Use the clues to complete the crossword with reporting nouns.

Across

6 information that people are talking about even though they don't know if it is true
7 new information
9 an answer to something that has been said
10 a brief remark
11 when you say something or someone is bad
12 when you say something that suggests what you think or want, but not in a direct way

Down

1 when someone says that they will hurt you, or cause problems for you if you don't do what they say
2 something that someone says or writes officially
3 when you say what will happen in the future
4 a statement or proof that something is true
5 a suggestion for a plan
8 when you admit that you've done something wrong or illegal

2 Choose the correct words to complete the sentences.

1 I wasn't happy with my coach's *response / threat* to my letter of complaint.
2 We have received *confirmation / confession* by email that the match starts at 3.30.
3 I don't know what to buy Maria for her birthday and she hasn't given me any *hint / rumour* about what she wants.
4 There was no *mention / prediction* of the tournament in any newspapers.
5 We're looking forward to the *proposal / update* on the progress the team has made so far.
6 My *hint / prediction* for tomorrow's match is a 4–0 win for us.
7 I thought that your *response / criticism* of the team's performance was very unfair.
8 The football club released an official *statement / confirmation* about the behaviour of their new manager.

3 Complete the sentences with the words in the box.

confession	criticism	threat
proposal	rumour	response

1 My coach's _____ to drop me from the team if I didn't train harder upset me – but it worked.
2 I have a _____ to make – I haven't trained for over a month.
3 Steven doesn't take _____ very well, so it's best not to say anything bad about his performance.
4 What is your _____ to people who question your commitment to the club?
5 Have you read the _____ for a new sports hall at school?
6 There's a _____ going around that you're leaving the club. Is it true?

Four Young Fans

A Elena Vlachou

The word 'fan' comes from the Latin word 'fanatic', which means 'a person whose enthusiasm for something is extreme'. In this sense, 15-year-old Elena Vlachou, from Athens, is most certainly a fan of her local basketball team AEK B.C. 'I live for them,' she tells us. All fans experience highs and lows depending on how their team is doing, and, fortunately for Elena, AEK B.C. don't often lose – so she's generally on a high. 'But the lows are pretty bad,' she says. Like many fans, Elena is quite superstitious, and follows a strict routine on match days, involving what she has for breakfast and the colour of her socks. 'It doesn't always work,' she confesses. But Elena is also loyal to the highly-successful AEK football club. So if the basketball team does badly, there's a good chance the football result will cheer her up!

B Riko Hanja

Although he lives in Korea, Riko Hanja has chosen to follow a team from the other side of the world: Manchester United Football Club. 'I've always loved football – both playing it and watching it – and Man U are really popular in my country. I can't remember when I didn't support them,' he says. He never misses a game on TV. His parents are also sports fans, so they subscribe to all the necessary channels. He's hoping that for his 18th birthday they'll take him to Manchester to watch the team play at their home stadium, Old Trafford. 'That would be amazing. There's a Man U fans' forum that I'm a part of where we chat about the matches and a couple of my friends on there have been to Manchester. They often mention it and I'm so jealous.' Good luck, Riko. We hope your dream comes true!

C Mark Lansman

Canadian teen Mark Lansman has always been crazy about ice hockey. It all started after a friend of the family took him to see the Montreal Canadiens vs. the Toronto Maple Leafs – and he was hooked from that moment on. 'The Maple Leafs won that day, and so I became a fan – even though we live in Montreal!' His decision caused a bit of friction at the time – literally everyone he knew was a Canadiens supporter – but Mark had made up his mind. 'I think they've come to terms with it now,' he tells us. Since then, he has become an accomplished player himself, representing his school and county as a goalkeeper. His ambition is to turn professional one day. 'I love it,' he says. 'When I'm at a Leaf's game, I get as excited as everyone else, but there's always a part of me that would rather be out there on the ice.'

D Clara Hanson

Going to an international sports event usually costs quite a lot of money, but lucky Clara Hanson came home from an England vs. India cricket match £1,000 richer. 'I caught the ball!' Clara explains. One of the match sponsors offers a large cash prize to anyone in the crowd who catches the ball before it hits the ground. It doesn't happen very often. 'I don't even play cricket,' says Clara. 'I'm just good at catching.' Although not a player, Clara has been a huge fan ever since her uncle took her to see his local team when she was seven. Now she goes to every game she can. She intends to use the prize money to travel to see the England team play in Australia next year. 'I want to get a really good job when I'm older, so that I can afford to follow them around the world when they're on tour.'

READING

1 Quickly read the article. Which sport is each young person a fanatic about?

2 Read the article again and write A, B, C or D for each question.

Which teenager ...

1 is interested in more than one sports team?
2 doesn't play the sport they like?
3 does the same thing before every game?
4 likes to discuss their team's performance online?
5 was introduced to the sport by a family member?
6 prefers playing the sport to watching it?
7 is hoping to have a career in sport?
8 has never seen their favourite team in real life?
9 gets in a bad mood when their team loses?
10 likes a different team from the rest of their family?

3 Match the highlighted words and phrases in the text to the definitions.

1 skilled or successful
2 always liking and supporting someone or something
3 a person or organisation that gives money to support an activity, event, etc.
4 pay money to an organisation in order to receive a product or use a service regularly
5 started liking something and wanted to do it all the time

1 Tick (✓) the correct statement.

1 Ivan said that he had been at the gym.
  A 'I'm at the gym.' ....
  B 'I've been at the gym.' ....

2 He claimed that nobody played the game better than he did.
  A 'Nobody plays the game better than I do.' ....
  B 'Nobody is playing the game better than I am.' ....

3 'I'll help you pack.'
  A She said she helped him pack. ....
  B She said she would help him pack. ....

4 He said he was practising for the following week's match.
  A 'I was practising for the following week's match.' ....
  B 'I'm practising for next week's match.' ....

5 'Hockey is a very physical sport.'
  A Alys said that hockey is a very physical sport. ....
  B Alys said that hockey had been a very physical sport. ....

2 Complete the reported statements.

1 'You did very well in the competition.'
  My coach said that I .... very well in the competition.

2 'I'll do my best.'
  Jenny said she .... best.

3 'He's currently the fastest cyclist in the world.'
  Maria said that he .... currently the fastest cyclist in the world.

4 'It isn't going to be a very exciting race.'
  Ben warned me that it .... to be a very exciting race.

5 'I don't want you to injure yourself today.'
  He said that he didn't want me to injure myself .... day.

3 Rewrite the direct speech statements in reported speech.

1 'I've decided to start taking driving lessons.'
  Laura said ....

2 'He never wanted to be team captain.'
  Alicia told me ....

3 'Training's always better in the morning.'
  Artur said ....

4 'I'm feeling exhausted after all that running.'
  Hannah complained ....

5 'They'll play much better with a new manager.'
  Peter argued ....

4 Correct the mistakes in four of the sentences. Which one is correct?

1 John said he had some good news to tell me.
....

2 She told me that she has to finish her homework then she could come to see me.
....

3 They told us that the shop will open the following week.
....

4 He rang me and said that we can meet later that day.
....

5 He told us that he can't come because something very urgent had happened.
....

1 Choose the best reporting verb in the box to report each statement. There are two extra verbs.

| admit | beg | ~~confirm~~ | declare |
| emphasise | propose | remind | reveal |

The rumours are true. <u>I have resigned as manager of the team</u>.

0 *confirm*

Please, please, <u>give me one more chance</u>.

1 ....

I think <u>we should enter both teams in the tournament</u>.

2 ....

Yes, <u>it was me who forgot to inform the referee that the match was cancelled</u>.

3 ....

Nobody knows this yet – <u>our new signing cost us €5 million</u>.

4 ....

Don't forget that <u>you need to go to your training session today</u>.

5 ....

2 Report the statements in Exercise 1 using the reporting verbs you chose. You only need to report the <u>underlined</u> words.

0 *He/She confirmed that he/she had resigned as manager of the team.*

1 ....

2 ....

3 ....

4 ....

5 ....

ACCIDENT-PRONE

Everyone has accidents from time to time. A bump on the head, a slip on a wet floor – it's almost impossible to go through life without suffering such minor events once in a while. But why do some people seem to suffer accidents more often than others?

1 .... 'I seem to have more accidents when I'm feeling stressed, or thinking about something,' says the 19-year-old computer programmer. 'Once I slipped on a wet kitchen floor and broke my wrist, and three days later I tripped over a step and hurt my shoulder. Then, the following week, a guitar fell on my head when I was opening a wardrobe. I'm sure these things all happened because I wasn't paying attention.'

2 .... She believes that people who are stressed aren't 'living in the present'. They're thinking about the future or about something that's happened in the past. That's why they aren't paying attention to what's going on around them. 'If you're busy, you go from task to task, and while you're doing one thing, you're thinking about what your next job is going to be,' she says. 'Or you might be thinking about a conversation you had earlier in the day, and wishing you had said something different. Either way, you're not living in the present. You're somewhere else. And that's when accidents happen.'

3 .... Recent research indicates that accident-prone people really do exist. Scientists in the Netherlands studied the accidents of nearly 150,000 people from different countries, and found that one out of every 29 people has a 50% or higher chance of having an accident than the rest of the population. So, does that suggest that these people are more stressed than the other 28 in every 29?

4 .... The scientists concluded that stress wasn't the main factor in causing accidents. 'Stress and anxiety don't help,' says Professor Kurt Knopf, 'but the biggest problem seems to be multitasking – trying to do more than one thing at a time. If you're chopping onions with a sharp knife, you have to concentrate on it. You can't let things like shouting children or a ringing telephone distract you, or you'll cut yourself.'

5 .... Take the sad case of Trevor Cookson. His life started badly, and it never got any better. He was accident-prone before he was even born, as his mother nearly lost him when she was pregnant. Then he suffered a lot of serious accidents as a child. He broke bones in the playground, and had to have a major operation when he was hurt playing rugby.

6 .... That didn't stop him going to university and studying law, though. After he graduated, he worked in a law firm where he had to travel a lot, and as a consequence, broke his back once in a car accident. However, he always managed to fight back to health. What's more, he never seemed to be particularly stressed or anxious about anything. In fact, he's now married to a nurse he met when in hospital after breaking his back. 'At least I'm there to look after him when he has another accident', says Simone, his wife, though he's managed the last few years without any accidents at all!

So next time you have an accident, think about Trevor Cookson. He never complained!

3 Choose the correct answer to complete the sentences.

1 Kirsty Ball *understands / doesn't understand* why she has so many accidents.
2 Danielle Mamby believes that people tend to have accidents *when they are very busy / when they are thinking about something else*.
3 Scientists believe that the main cause of accidents is *anxiety / lack of concentration*.
4 Trevor Cookson had a lot of accidents because *he was unlucky / he had a stressful life*.

4 Match the highlighted words in the article to the definitions.

1 more important, bigger or more serious than others of the same type ....
2 the feeling of being very worried ....
3 the part of the body between the hand and the arm ....
4 not important or serious ....
5 likely to experience a particular problem more often than is usual ....

1 Put the words in the correct order to make reported questions and requests.

1 was / it / she / him / what time / asked

2 to know / warm enough / he / if / was / I / wanted

3 speak / asked / the headteacher / to / my mother / to

4 they / the kids / where / the police officer / had / been / asked

5 asked / to help / my sister / me / her

6 where / the man / me / staying / asked / I / was

2 Complete the reported questions and requests.

1 'What time did you wake up?'
She asked him what time he

2 'Please phone for an ambulance.'
The man asked the driver

3 'Have you started your project yet?'
The teacher asked her

4 'When are we leaving?'
She asked him when they

5 'Are we all going to the park?'
He asked her if they

6 'Can you help me get out of the car?'
The driver asked the police officer

7 'Did you hear that strange noise?'
I asked him if he

8 'What were you doing when it happened?'
She asked him what he

9 'Can you help me to get up, please?'
The old lady who had fallen asked me

10 'What has happened in this room?'
Mum came in and asked us

3 Write the direct speech of the reported questions and requests in the speech bubbles.

Do you like my new bike?

0 He asked her if she liked his new bike.
1 She asked him where he had bought it.

2 She asked him to make her a sandwich.
3 He asked her if she had eaten her lunch.

4 He asked her to pick him up.
5 She asked him where he was.

6 She asked him if she could borrow a pencil.
7 He asked her what colour she wanted.

4 Correct the mistakes in three of the sentences. Which two are correct?

1 She told me that she was with some friends in a restaurant and she told everyone what they wanted for lunch.

2 Secondly, you asked me to inform you about our club.

3 I was not sure about the decision I should make, so I asked my family what I should do.

4 Angela asked Mark what was the strange light.

5 I wanted to know how could I get the magazines or newspapers.

1 Match the phrases to the meanings.

1 make fun of ....
2 make a promise ....
3 have a word ....
4 give someone a hug ....
5 have a quarrel/an argument ....
6 have the strength ....
7 give someone a hand ....
8 make a call ....
9 make an attempt ....
10 give a talk ....

a talk to someone for a short time
b make a joke about someone or something in an unkind way
c put your arms around someone and hold them tightly
d say that you will certainly do something
e help
f disagree strongly with someone
g be strong enough
h try to do something
i telephone someone
j give a presentation on a particular topic to a group of people

2 Complete the second sentence so that it has a similar meaning to the first sentence, using the word given. Do not change the word given. You must use between two and five words, including the word given.

0 The doctor spoke briefly to the nurse and then came to my bed.
   WORD
   Before she came to my bed, the doctor
   ___*had a word*___ with the nurse.

1 Martha asked for help carrying her suitcase.
   HAND
   'Can someone _____ with my suitcase?' said Martha.

2 When I won the race, my coach hugged me.
   GAVE
   My coach _____ when I won the race.

3 'I'll never ride without a helmet again,' Mark promised.
   MADE
   Mark _____ never to ride without a helmet again.

4 I'm still much too weak to go back to school.
   STRENGTH
   I _____ to go back to school yet.

5 I've never seen my parents argue about anything.
   ARGUMENT
   As far as I know, my parents have _____ about anything.

6 Phone the hospital if you think you're seriously ill.
   MAKE
   If you think you're seriously ill, _____ to the hospital.

 07

1 You will hear people talking in eight different situations. For questions 1–8, choose the best answer.

1 You hear a boy talking about a road accident he was in.
   Why did he crash?
   A The road conditions were unsafe.
   B Another road user made a mistake.
   C He was feeling angry about something.

2 You hear two friends talking about a clothes shop.
   What does the boy think his friend will dislike about it?
   A the price of the clothes there
   B the people who work there
   C the music they play there

3 You hear a girl talking about how she broke her tooth.
   How does she feel about the accident?
   A disappointed by her own carelessness
   B annoyed at her brothers for distracting her
   C relieved that no permanent damage was done

4 You hear a man and a woman talking on the radio.
   What point is the man making about life in the 21st century?
   A People seldom relax properly.
   B People are too easily frightened.
   C People are lucky to have lots of things to do.

5 You hear a woman talking about a skiing accident she had.
   She believes she injured herself because
   A her instructor encouraged her to take a risk.
   B she lost concentration at the last moment.
   C she was overconfident about her skills.

6 You hear a boy and a girl talking about a trip on a boat.
   What does the boy say about the trip?
   A It was too expensive.
   B It was too scary.
   C It was too long.

7 You hear a girl talking on the phone to her father.
   What is the purpose of her call?
   A to request some help
   B to borrow some money
   C to apologise for being late

8 You hear a boy and a girl talking in a café.
   They agree that
   A the drinks are really good.
   B the place looks good.
   C it is expensive.

15 TELLING THE TRUTH

1 Match the expressions and actions to the situations.

1 You bite your lip	....	**a** when you're tired.
2 You lick your lips	....	**b** when you don't stop looking at them.
3 You nod your head	....	**c** when you feel nervous.
4 You shake your head	....	**d** when you don't want to start a conversation with them.
5 You yawn	....	**e** when you are about to eat something delicious.
6 You blush	....	**f** when you agree.
7 You blink	....	**g** when you're embarrassed.
8 You rub your eyes	....	**h** when they're tired or itchy.
9 You stare at someone	....	**i** when you disagree.
10 You avoid eye contact with someone	....	**j** when you suddenly see a bright light, or you have something in your eye.

2 Choose the correct options to complete the sentences.

1 I was really worried about my sister when she was ill, but I .... and tried not to show my feelings.
  A bit my lip   **B** licked my lips

2 'Yes, I'll come to the party,' she said, ... her head enthusiastically.
  A shaking   **B** nodding

3 It had been such a long day that he couldn't stop ....
  A nodding   **B** yawning

4 I .... my head sadly when my mum asked me if I'd won any prizes that day.
  A shook   **B** nodded

5 Harry .... eagerly at the smells coming out of the kitchen.
  A bit his lips   **B** licked his lips

6 She .... when she got the answer wrong.
  A blushed   **B** yawned

7 Joe was in class, but I .... because we'd had a huge quarrel the day before.
  A stared at him   **B** avoided eye contact with him

8 Her eyes were red because she had been .... them.
  A rubbing   **B** blinking

9 Why is that strange little girl .... me? I don't know her!
  A staring at   **B** avoiding eye contact with

10 'Try not to .... while I'm doing the eye examination,' said the doctor.
  A stare   **B** blink

READING

1 Quickly read the article on page 61. Choose the best title.

  A Why lying is bad for you
  B How to lie effectively
  C Lying – the good news and the bad news

2 Six sentences have been removed from the article. Choose from the sentences A–G the one which fits each gap (1–6). There is one extra sentence which you do not need to use.

  A Just a few years later, we're pretty good at it – and do it several times a day.
  B It depends on how big the lie is.
  C However, not everyone develops the skill of effective lying.
  D In fact, even the most honest of us do it at least once a day.
  E Big lies, on the other hand, should be avoided.
  F But of course, it's not all good news.
  G We even lie to ourselves, which can have some positive effects.

Let's be honest: you've told some little white lies, haven't you?

Maybe you told your sister her new dress looked great when you really thought it was horrible. Perhaps you told your teacher you left your homework on the kitchen table when the truth was you forgot to do it. Or maybe you told your friend that you couldn't go out because you were busy when in fact you just didn't want to go out.

A However, you shouldn't feel too bad about it. You're not alone! Research shows that people lie all the time. [1] ____ Scientists have suggested lying might be necessary for society to work properly – and, in some cases, it might even be good for you.

B We learn how to lie at a very young age. Our first experiments with lying happen at around the age of three. [2] ____ It is believed that children learn to lie by observing their parents do it. Sometimes, parents even encourage children to lie – it's often just a case of teaching good manners: 'Thank you for my present. I love it!' and 'That was delicious.' are two common examples.

C There are many other reasons why we tell lies, apart from politeness. Maybe we want to get some kind of reward or advantage, for example, or maybe we want to protect someone from getting their feelings hurt. [3] ____ People who boast about their abilities in something – even if those abilities are not so great – often improve faster than those who are more realistic in their self-assessment.

D [4] ____ If you're deceiving yourself to an unrealistic level, it can have a damaging effect on your confidence when you fail. If your innocent and polite lies to others are discovered, that can have a terrible effect on your relationships because you will no longer be trusted. Even if your little white lie is not discovered, knowing that you've told it can damage your own self-image as a good and honest person, making you feel bad.

E So how can you tell if someone is lying to you? [5] ____ Little white lies, such as 'That was a lovely meal,' are hard to detect, because they're easy to tell. But when someone tells a serious lie, especially if they aren't used to lying, their heart rate and body temperature may increase. They may also appear very nervous.

To sum up, there are both positive and negative things about lying. Ultimately, the little lies we tell every day probably do more good than harm, provided they are told well enough not to make anyone suspicious. [6] ____ Although they may produce advantages in the short term, the damage they do to your sense of self-worth is a high price to pay. And that price gets much higher if you develop a reputation for being a liar!

3 Answer the questions.

Which paragraph (A–E) …
1 gives an example of how lying can help us improve? ....
2 informs us that lying is common? ....
3 lists some bad consequences of lying? ....
4 compares some kinds of lying with being polite? ....
5 looks at two kinds of lying and their effect on us? ....

4 Match the highlighted words in the text to the definitions.

1 the opinion that people have about someone based on their behaviour or character in the past ....
2 talk with too much pride about what you have done or what you own ....
3 polite ways of behaving with other people ....
4 discover or notice something, especially something that is difficult to see, hear, smell, etc. ....
5 making someone believe something that is not true ....

1 Complete the sentences with the correct form of the verbs in the box.

bring	cut	feed	~~fix~~	install
publish	steal	test		

0 I got my uncle _____*to fix*_____ my broken bike wheel – he's good at things like that.

1 Mum had her car _____ when she left it at the station overnight.

2 What time are you having your hair _____ this afternoon?

3 He was very happy when he had his letter _____ in the local newspaper.

4 We're going to get our neighbour _____ our fish while we're on holiday.

5 My rich aunt likes to have her breakfast _____ to her room when she stays in a hotel.

6 That referee should have his eyes _____!

7 We had a new bathroom _____ in our house last month.

2 Put the words in the correct order to make sentences.

1 broken / our front window / had / last night / we

2 got / the teacher / to tidy / after school / the classroom / the students

3 by a dog / Liam / his arm / bitten / had

4 a doctor / should / to check / you / your eyes / get

5 had / we / painted / last week / our living room

6 in my project / getting / the spelling / my dad / I'm / to check

7 had / bright blue / her fingernails / painted / has / Pilar

8 load the dishwasher / us / Mum / gets / to / after breakfast / always

3 Complete the answers to the questions with the correct form of *have something done* or *get someone to do something*. Sometimes both are possible.

1 Does she cut her own hair?
No, she _____ at the hairdresser's.

2 Did you wrap all those presents yourself?
No, I _____ them for me.

3 Is Tim going to design his own webpage?
No, he _____ it for him.

4 Do you fix your own bike?
No, I _____ at the bike shop.

5 Is Tina going to make her own wedding dress?
No, she _____ by a professional.

6 Do you iron your own clothes?
No, I _____ them for me.

4 Tick (✓) the correct sentences.

1 A She took me to the hospital, where the doctor told me that I had my leg broken.
B She took me to the hospital, where the doctor told me that I had broken my leg.

2 A I prefer working with the animals, but I know how hard it is to get someone to help in the office.
B I prefer working with the animals, but I know how hard it is to get someone to helping in the office.

3 A I took her by her shoulders for her to stop yelling for a while.
B I took her by her shoulders to get her to stop yelling for a while.

4 A A car is quite expensive and it costs money every time you have it repaired.
B A car is quite expensive and it costs money every time you have it to be repaired.

5 A You can make more people to take part by holding swimming competitions.
B You can get more people to take part by holding swimming competitions.

1 Choose the correct words to complete the sentences.

1 We had to fix our flat tyre *itself / ourselves*.
2 That day, Ben and Ellie met the president *himself / ourselves*.
3 My grandparents built this house *myself / themselves*.
4 Stephanie makes all her clothes *herself / themselves*.
5 I will finish this project *itself / myself*.
6 Tidy your room *himself / yourself*, you lazy boy.
7 We didn't get to see the Eiffel Tower *ourselves / itself* – just a model of it.
8 Did you and your brother decorate this whole room *itself / yourselves*?

2 Match 1–6 to a–f.

1 Who cooked dinner for you?   ....
2 Make me a sandwich.   ....
3 Who tidied your brothers' room?   ....
4 Nobody is going to help us.   ....
5 Sally looks such a mess.   ....
6 It was an interesting exhibition.   ....

a She shouldn't cut her hair herself.
b I met the photographer himself afterwards.
c Do it yourself.
d I did it myself.
e They did it themselves.
f We have to do it ourselves.

1 Look at the exam task. Then answer questions 1–4 with your own ideas for a possible story.

> **Stories wanted!**
> Would you like to have your story published on our website? Enter our competition! Your story must begin with this sentence:
> *When I got up on Saturday morning, I checked my phone and saw the text.*
> Your story must include:
> • an arrangement
> • a gift

Write your **story**.

1 What did the text say?

....

2 Who wrote it?

....

3 What happened next?

....

4 How did you feel?

....

2 Read the story. Is it similar to your notes in Exercise 1?

When I got up on Saturday morning, I checked my phone and saw the text. It said, 'Please meet me outside the library at four o'clock. Don't be late!'

The text was from Jim, a classmate from my old school. We used to be good friends, but we had a quarrel and stopped talking to each other. I thought Jim had stolen my tennis racket from my sports locker, but Jim denied it. It's hard to stay friends when you don't trust each other.

But I was curious about why he wanted to see me now. It was over a year since we last spoke. So I got my coat and caught the bus into town. When I got to the library, Jim was waiting for me. 'I want to apologise to you,' he said – and he handed me a brand new tennis racket! 'I did take your tennis racket a year ago, and I'm sorry I lied.'

Although I was still a bit angry with Jim for lying to me, I was happy about the new tennis racket. We're friends again now, and play tennis together every weekend.

3 Answer the questions about the story.

1 What did the message say? ....
2 Who wrote it? ....
3 What happened next? ....
4 What was the lie? ....
5 What was the gift? ....
6 How did the writer feel? ....

4 Choose the best title for the story.

A Never trust a liar
B Forgive and forget
C Time heals everything

5 Write a story for the task in Exercise 1. Use your notes in Exercise 1 and the questions in Exercise 3 to help you. Write 140–190 words.

16 WHO CARES?

Climate change

1 Put the letters in the correct order to make climate change phrases.

1 b o n c a r i d e d i o x s i o n s e m i s _____
2 n o b r c a o o t r i n t f p _____
3 r g y e n e c i e n t e f f i _____
4 t a l l y r o n m e n e n v i d l y e f r i n _____
5 e u s t x h a u s f m e _____
6 s i l f o s e l s f u _____
7 b a l g l o m i n g w a r _____
8 u s e e n h g r e o g s a s e _____
9 w a b l e r e n e r g y e n e r c e s s o u _____
10 a r s o l w o p e r _____
11 n d w i w e r p o _____

2 Complete the table with the phrases in Exercise 1.

Good for the planet	Bad for the planet
	carbon dioxide emissions

3 Choose the correct options to complete the text.

We've just had a lesson on climate change at school. Mr Green explained how using forms of transport which produce a lot of [1]*carbon dioxide emissions / carbon footprint* isn't environmentally friendly, and is causing [2]*fossil fuels / global warming*. Not only that, but [3]*exhaust fumes / renewable energy sources* in cities are causing a lot of ill-health in the population. But he said things were getting better. Cars are becoming much more energy efficient, and electric cars are becoming more popular. They use less [4]*global warming / fossil fuel* – and the electricity they use is increasingly being produced by [5]*renewable energy sources / exhaust fumes* in the form of [6]*carbon dioxide emissions / solar power*. So it's not all bad news!

1 Read the first two paragraphs of an article and decide which answer (A, B, C or D) best fits each gap.

SIX surprising results of climate change

1 Most people have a general idea about what global warming [0] *involves*. After all, the data that shows rising temperatures and [1]_____ ice caps is there for all to see. Sea [2]_____ are rising at a rate of about four millimetres per year. That may not sound like much, but the Earth's changing climate is already [3]_____ problems.

2 Not [4]_____ is global warming shrinking glaciers and creating more powerful hurricanes, but it also seems to be causing more forest fires than ever before. Recent wildfires in the western USA have both covered more ground and [5]_____ for longer. Their increased size and frequency mean that firefighters have a much harder time putting them [6]_____. What is more, there is a [7]_____ relationship between the warmer temperatures and the early arrival of spring. When the snow disappears, forest [8]_____ become drier and stay dry for longer, which increases the chance that they might catch fire.

0	A includes	B involves	C requires	D concerns
1	A melting	B dropping	C fading	D dissolving
2	A heights	B measures	C lengths	D levels
3	A causing	B making	C resulting	D proving
4	A just	B only	C really	D alone
5	A stayed	B taken	C lasted	D rested
6	A off	B out	C over	D down
7	A clear	B straight	C simple	D clean
8	A fields	B parts	C places	D areas

3 PHOTO ____

All over the world, temples, ancient monuments and other statues stand as reminders of civilisations past, which until now have survived the tests of time. However the immediate effects of global warming may finally destroy them. Rising seas and extreme weather have the potential to damage these unique sites. Floods caused by global warming have already damaged Sukhothai – the 600-year-old site which was the ancient capital of a Thai kingdom.

4 PHOTO ____

The average climber probably wouldn't notice, but the Alps and other mountain ranges have experienced gradual growth over the past century or so thanks to the melting of the glaciers on top of them. For thousands of years, the weight of these glaciers has pushed the mountains down into the earth, squeezing them down like a cushion. As the glaciers melt, this weight is decreasing, and the surface is slowly rising. Global warming speeds up the melting of these glaciers, so the mountains are growing faster!

5 PHOTO ____

One hundred and twenty-five lakes in the Arctic have disappeared in the past few decades, giving support to the idea that global warming is working extremely fast nearest the Earth's poles. Research into the missing water points to the probability that frozen earth underneath the lakes warmed up and became soft – or thawed. As this normally permanently-frozen ground thaws, the water in the lakes can escape through the soil, draining the lakes. One researcher compared it to pulling the plug out of the bath.

6 PHOTO ____

While melting ice in the Arctic might cause problems for plants and animals further south, it's creating a bright and sunny situation for Arctic vegetation. Arctic plants are usually trapped in ice for most of the year. Now in spring, when the ice melts earlier, the plants start growing quickly. There has been an explosion of plant growth in the Arctic in recent decades!

7 PHOTO ____

Have those itchy eyes and sneezing fits that bother you every spring got worse in recent years? Global warming may be partly to blame for that, too. Over the past few decades, an increasing number of people have started suffering from seasonal allergies and asthma. Just like in the Arctic, early springs mean plants come into flower more quickly, so your allergy season can last longer. Better buy some more tissues!

2 Read the rest of the article and match paragraphs 3–7 to photos A–E.

3 Answer the questions about the article.

1 Why do early springs make forest fires more likely?

2 What caused the damage to an ancient site in Thailand?

3 Why are mountains getting higher?

4 What is the cause of the 'explosion of plant growth' in the Arctic?

5 How does climate change affect people with allergies?

4 Match the highlighted words in the text to the definitions.

1 having an uncomfortable feeling on the body which makes you want to scratch ____

2 when something increases suddenly by a large amount ____

3 something that makes you remember something else ____

4 agreement with an idea, group or person ____

5 happening slowly over a period of time ____

1 Match the beginnings and ends of the sentences.

1 I'd tour the world on a bicycle ....
2 If I were rich, ...
3 I could help you with your project ....
4 If I wasn't busy this weekend, ...
5 I wouldn't go to school every day ....
6 If recycling wasn't so important, ...

a I'd buy an expensive car.
b if I could get enough time off work.
c if you wanted me to.
d I might go to the cinema.
e I wouldn't do it.
f if I didn't have to.

2 Complete the second conditional sentences with the verbs in brackets. Sometimes more than one modal verb (*could, would* or *might*) is possible.

1 If we .... (recycle) more glass and paper, we .... (save) more energy.
2 Those noisy kids .... (go) outside if the weather .... (not be) so bad. Who knows!
3 You .... (do) better in your exams if you .... (work) a bit harder.
4 He .... (write) to her if he .... (know) her email address.
5 If we .... (not have) to go to school today, we .... (go) to the beach or maybe to the park.
6 If she .... (stop) using her tablet an hour before going to bed, she .... (sleep) better. It's worth trying.
7 We .... (be) lost if we .... (not have) our mobile phones with us.
8 Global warming .... (be) slowed if all the governments in the world .... (make) an effort. They should try at least!
9 It .... (be) much easier to recycle all our rubbish if we .... (have) different bins for everything.
10 If I .... (work) every Saturday morning from now to my exams, I .... (be) able to go on holiday with my friends in the summer. It's a possibility.
11 If Maria .... (smile) and .... (chat) a bit more with people, she .... (make) more friends.
12 Mum and Dad always say we .... (save) thousands if my brother and I .... (turn) off the lights more often!

3 Complete the sentences with the correct form of the words in the box.

| be / rich   be / sunny   can / get to sleep |
| ~~have / an umbrella~~   not be / closed |
| not play / loud music   speak / Chinese |

0 It's pouring down. I wish *I had an umbrella.*
1 I'd love a Ferrari. If only ....
2 I'm so worried about the test tomorrow. If only ....
3 We'd love to go to the beach today. If only ....
4 Oh, I'm too late to do the shopping. I wish the supermarket ....
5 I don't understand a word on this holiday. I wish ....
6 These new neighbours are nice, but I wish ....

4 Correct the mistakes in four of the sentences. Which one is correct?

1 If everyone stops using so much plastic, climate change might slow down.

2 I would be grateful if you correct your errors.

3 I wish you will send me the answers.

4 I can't afford to go to the concert. If only I had more money!

5 There's not a lot for young people to do, so it could be good if you invented something!

1 Choose the correct options to complete the sentences.

1 *Assuming / Even if* more wind farms are built in the next few years, electricity should get cheaper.
2 She wouldn't invite him to her party *assuming / even if* he asked her.
3 I'll buy some new trainers *as long as / even if* they aren't too expensive.
4 You may go to the pool without an adult *provided that / even if* you are over 14 years old.
5 *As long as / Even if* we had enough oil to last another 100 years, we should still try to find alternative forms of energy.
6 You'll save a lot of electricity *as long as / even if* you follow the recommendations in this article.

1 Look at the photo of young environmental activists. What sort of things does an environmental activist do?

2 You will hear an interview with a young environmental activist and author called Darren Gibbons. For questions 1–7, choose the best answer (A, B or C).

1 Why did Darren become involved in environmental issues?
A His parents encouraged him to be active.
B He followed the example of his friends.
C He was influenced by a TV show.

2 Darren wrote the book in order to
A encourage young people to change their habits.
B help young people organise themselves more effectively.
C improve the environment around his home.

3 Darren believes his book is
A not selling many copies.
B not very well written.
C not very original.

4 How does Darren feel about the media attention he attracts?
A He accepts it as part of his activism.
B He is annoyed by the attitude of interviewers.
C He is suspicious of the motives of journalists.

5 When Darren gives talks to schoolchildren, he
A is encouraged by the interest they show.
B feels nervous about making mistakes.
C enjoys making them laugh.

6 Darren believes that young environmental activists should
A be careful not to lose sight of the big picture.
B find like-minded people to support them.
C concentrate on making small changes around them.

7 How does Darren feel about the future?
A optimistic that things will improve
B determined to continue campaigning
C confident that more people will join him

3 Listen again and check your answers in Exercise 2.

17 ART IS FUN!

VOCABULARY — Adjectives describing art

1 Complete the adjectives with the missing vowels.

1 cl___ss___c
2 c___ntr___v___rs_____l
3 b___z___rr___
4 dr___m___t___c
5 r___m___rk___bl
6 st___nn___ng
7 p___w___rf___l
8 h___m___r_____s
9 ___n___q___
10 ___bstr___ct
11 c___nt___mp___r___ry
12 c___nv___nt_____n___l

2 Match the adjectives in Exercise 1 to their meanings.

1 very sudden or noticeable, or full of action and excitement ....
2 very unusual or noticeable in a way that you admire ....
3 having all the characteristics or qualities that you expect ....
4 having a strong effect on people ....
5 very strange and unusual ....
6 different from everyone and everything else ....
7 very beautiful and attractive ....
8 existing or happening now ....
9 causing disagreement or discussion ....
10 funny, or making you laugh ....
11 involving shapes and colours and not images of real things or people ....
12 traditional and ordinary ....

3 Choose the correct words to complete the sentences.

1 I don't really like ...... art – I prefer to look at pictures of real things.
   A humorous **B** abstract **C** dramatic
2 He's a very ...... artist, whose work makes some people angry.
   A controversial **B** classic **C** dramatic
3 I've never seen anything quite like this ...... painting.
   A conventional **B** contemporary **C** remarkable
4 Do you prefer ...... art, or older more traditional paintings?
   A classic **B** contemporary **C** dramatic
5 Nobody else paints like this artist – her work is ....
   A dramatic **B** classic **C** unique
6 His work is not very interesting or adventurous – in fact, it's boringly ....
   A bizarre **B** conventional **C** dramatic
7 This piece is simply ...... – I've never seen anything so beautiful.
   A controversial **B** classic **C** stunning
8 I don't know if this painting is deliberately ...... , but it certainly makes me laugh!
   A humorous **B** conventional **C** abstract

READING

1 Look at the example of graffiti art on page 69. What makes it different from more traditional forms of art?

....
....

2 Read the first paragraph of the article. For questions 1–8, think of the word which best fits each gap. Use only one word in each gap.

BANKSY, WHO ARE YOU?

For years, his artwork ⁰ _has_ mysteriously appeared on walls and buildings ¹ _____ the world. But nobody knows who he is. Indeed, the ten-year mission to discover the true identity of the graffiti artist ² _____ as 'Banksy' has become almost as fascinating as the controversial artwork itself. There are very ³ _____ things about him we can be sure about, ⁴ _____ as the fact that he comes from Bristol and his first name is Robin – but that's about it. Several years ago, a national newspaper claimed to have ⁵ _____ out the name of the artist using a photograph which apparently showed him ⁶ _____ work. The newspaper contacted several of his friends, ⁷ _____ all identified the man in the picture as Robin Gunningham, an ex-pupil from an expensive private school in Bristol. The artist's agents refused to confirm ⁸ _____ Mr Gunningham was Banksy or not. 'We get these calls all the time,' said his spokesman.

Since Banksy became a major street artist, his work has sold for thousands of pounds. People who have bought Banksy artwork include the actor Angelina Jolie and the singer Christina Aguilera. He's certainly fashionable!

His journey to fame is a remarkable one. One of the first conventional exhibitions of his art was held in 2000, but the mysterious Banksy gave out only the number of the building and not the name of the street. Nevertheless, interest in him began to grow. He developed strategies to keep his identity secret, like doing interviews only on the phone and using trusted business colleagues to handle sales.

As his fame grew, so did the danger of being caught spraying his unique graffiti on public walls. He began to think up more complex and unusual stunts. For example, he got into the penguin exhibit at London Zoo and painted 'We're bored of fish' on the wall. Then in October 2003, he

hung one of his own paintings in the famous Tate Gallery in London. Then he did a similar thing in 2005 at four major museums in New York City. One of those museums – the Museum of Modern Art – decided to add the piece to their permanent collection. More recently, he put his famous *Girl with Balloon* painting up for auction in London. It was held in a specially made frame which shredded the painting as soon as it was sold – for £1,042,000. Fortunately for the buyer, this act of destruction actually doubled its value!

When Banksy does agree to give an interview, he ensures that the public never discover his true identity. 'I have no interest in ever coming out,' he told an arts magazine. 'I'm just trying to make the pictures look good; I'm not into trying to make myself look good. And besides, it's a pretty safe bet that the reality of me would be a crushing disappointment to a couple of 15-year-old kids out there.'

3 Read the rest of the article. Are the sentences *T* (True), *F* (False) or *NM* (Not Mentioned)?

1 Banksy's agents frequently deal with enquiries about his identity. ....
2 Very few people turned up to Banksy's first exhibition. ....
3 Banksy doesn't care about people knowing his real name. ....
4 Banksy employs people to look after the business side of his art. ....
5 A museum in the USA kept one of Banksy's paintings to display to visitors. ....
6 Banksy says that he will one day reveal his identity to the world. ....

4 Match the highlighted words in the text to the definitions.

1 cut into thin strips ....
2 say or show that something is true ....
3 makes certain to happen ....
4 involving a lot of different but connected parts in a way that is difficult to understand ....
5 strange or unknown, and not explained or understood ....

1 Complete the sentences with *must* or *can't*.

1 Look at all those football trophies. She _____ be a really good player.
2 She isn't answering the door. She _____ be at home.
3 He has a strong Chinese accent. He _____ be from China.
4 You've just had lunch. You _____ be hungry!
5 They haven't had a drink all afternoon. They _____ be thirsty.
6 He lives in a big house. He _____ be rich.
7 Nobody is buying her cakes. They _____ taste very nice.
8 She's got a lot of books. She _____ love reading.

2 Choose the correct modal verbs to complete the sentences.

1 Dan and Michael _____ be in the same class, but I'm not sure.
   A can't   B must   C could
2 That _____ be Amanda in the shop. She's on holiday.
   A can't   B mustn't   C could
3 You _____ be right – you often are.
   A can't   B might well   C must
4 This _____ be the best picture you've ever painted! It's stunning.
   A could well   B can well   C can't
5 This _____ be the first time you've seen this film – it's been out for ages!
   A could   B mustn't   C can't
6 The shops _____ be closed by now, I'm not sure. What time do they close on Thursdays?
   A can't   B could   C must

3 Complete the second sentence so that it has a similar meaning to the first sentence. Use the word in brackets.

1 I'm sure my keys are in this room somewhere! (must)
   My keys _____
2 Sonja definitely isn't from France. (can't)
   Sonja _____
3 It seems quite likely that Lisa likes Noah. (well)
   Lisa _____
4 It's possible that Tom doesn't play rugby. (might)
   Tom _____
5 Jane is in Mexico, so I'm certain that isn't her on the bus. (be)
   That _____
6 Surely you aren't serious about wanting to be an astronaut. (joking)
   You _____

4 Correct the mistakes in two of the sentences. Which three are correct?

1 Both talks must be very interesting.

2 It could be difficult for me.

3 She thinks that the computer takes too much time and that it can be harmful for my health.

4 It mustn't be very nice for the animals to be disturbed all day and to have no freedom.

5 You must be the tourists from England.

1 Choose the correct verbs to complete the sentences.

1 The president of our club was _____ last year.
   A influenced   B elected   C prohibited
2 When was this university _____?
   A established   B awarded   C devoted
3 The entire first floor of the building was _____ to the art exhibition.
   A elected   B set   C devoted
4 I was _____ by my father in my decision to study music.
   A influenced   B composed   C regarded
5 Our team was _____ a silver medal in the volleyball tournament.
   A elected   B awarded   C entitled

2 Rewrite the sentences using the passive form of the verbs in the box.

~~award~~	compose	entitle
prohibit	regard	set

0 The school gave Maria a prize for her work with younger pupils.
   Maria was awarded a prize for her work with younger pupils.
1 They don't allow ball games in this park.

2 A tiny island is the location for this novel.

3 People think Banksy is a good artist.

4 *Art in the City* is the name of the TV programme.

5 The final concert consisted of five bands, each playing for half an hour.

1 Read the essay title. Imagine how you would answer the question. Write brief notes below for points 1 and 2 in the task box. Then write one of your own ideas.

> **'Art is not a subject which should be taught in schools.'**
> **Do you agree?**
>
> **Notes**
> Write about:
> 1 how useful it is to learn about art
> 2 having enough time for other subjects
> 3 .... (your own idea)

1 ....
  ....

2 ....
  ....

3 ....
  ....

2 Read the essay quickly. Are any of your ideas from Exercise 1 mentioned?

....

> 1 On the other hand, there are people who believe that art is useless. They may believe that the purpose of education is to produce people who can create wealth for the country by helping businesses to grow and making useful things. To these people, time spent teaching art is time wasted when teachers could be teaching other more practical subjects.
> 2 Some people would argue that art is a useful subject because it is an important part of life. It helps us to understand the world, therefore it should be included in the education system. A world without art would be very boring indeed.
> 3 In my view, art is a very important part of our culture. I believe that it should always be taught in schools.
> 4 This is a very controversial question. Nearly all schools teach art to their students, but are there any reasons why they should not?
> 5 However, I think these people are wrong. Artists can create wealth by selling their works, so it is not a waste of time. For example, Banksy is probably very wealthy. What is more, he attracts visitors to the country.

3 Read the essay again and match the paragraphs to the functions.

a .... (introduction)
b .... (discussion of the first idea in the essay question)
c .... (discussion of the second idea in the essay question)
d .... (your idea)
e .... (conclusion)

4 Match the highlighted words and phrases in the essay to the words and phrases with a similar meaning below.

0 Despite this, *However,*
1 Some might say ....
2 For this reason, ...
3 For instance, ...
4 In contrast, ...
5 In my opinion, ...
6 Furthermore, ...
7 I think ....

5 Read the essay title. Then write notes in your notebook for each heading 1–3.

> **'Graffiti is not art, it is a crime.'**
> **Do you agree?**
>
> **Notes**
> Write about:
> 1 why graffiti is common
> 2 its effect on public spaces
> 3 .... (your own idea)

6 Write your essay in 140–190 words. Use the plan in Exercise 3 and linking words and phrases in Exercise 4.

18 CHALLENGING FATE

Personal qualities: nouns

1 Use the clues to complete the crossword with personal quaility nouns.

Across
5 a very powerful feeling, for example love, hate or anger
7 when someone continues trying to do something, although it is very difficult
9 energy and motivation to achieve things
10 the ability to do things that need a lot of physical effort or power

Down
1 someone or something that makes you feel that you want to do something and can do it
2 a strong feeling that you want to be successful or powerful
3 when you are willing to give your time and energy to something that you believe in
4 the quality of being generous, helpful, and thinking about other people's feelings
6 the ability to deal with a dangerous or difficult situation without being frightened
8 good judgement, especially about practical things

2 Choose the correct words to complete the sentences.

1 She has the *kindness / drive* to reach the very top of her profession.
2 I really appreciate your *kindness / courage* – that was very generous of you.
3 The team lacks *kindness / spirit* in the way it plays, and so is unlikely to win anything this season.
4 It takes a lot of *commitment / sense* and hard work to be a top athlete.
5 She showed real *courage / ambition* to get up on stage and speak to the crowd like that.
6 My father was my *spirit / inspiration* to take up singing professionally.

3 Complete the sentences with words from Exercise 1.

1 You need a lot of physical _____ to be a fightfighter because they need to be able to climb and lift heavy equipment.
2 My grandfather was given a medal for his _____ during the war.
3 We were all impressed by Susanna's _____ when she gave her prize money to a children's charity.
4 Usain Bolt was a real _____ to many young athletes. He's the reason many people took up running.
5 Luke's strong _____ and love for animals inspired his decision to become a vet.
6 I hope she has the _____ to stop training when she's ill, otherwise the exercise might do more harm than good.

READING

1 Look at the title of the article on page 73. What does the phrase 'from rags to riches' mean?

_____

2 Read the questions and underline the key words.

Which person …

1 has a brother or sister in the same field of business?
2 was successful at school?
3 got their biggest idea when on a journey?
4 was the youngest child in their family?
5 worked abroad before becoming famous?
6 has also worked as an actor?
7 was raised in several different households?
8 makes money in the fashion industry?
9 was trained by someone who later became an opponent?
10 was the first in their profession to become a billionaire?

3 For questions 1–10 in Exercise 2, choose from the texts (A–D) on page 73.

FROM RAGS TO RICHES

Four people who overcame challenges to become big successes in their field.

A OPRAH WINFREY

Born in rural Mississippi to an unmarried teenage mother, Oprah Winfrey did not have the easiest start in life. Until the age of six, she was looked after by her grandmother while her mother worked as a maid in another town. Throughout her childhood, she and her younger sister were moved around from relative to relative until, as a teenager, Oprah settled with her father. He made sure she got an education and Oprah shone in her lessons, even winning prizes for public speaking. This attracted the attention of a local radio station, where she worked as a news reader during her senior year. This was her first break into media. In 1983, she got a job hosting a TV talk show in Chicago which soon became the most successful talk-show in the USA because her kindness and humour appealed to audiences. Since then, Winfrey has become the first black female billionaire, authored five books, and had roles in several Hollywood films.

B J. K. ROWLING

The first person to become a billionaire through writing books, J. K. Rowling rose from poverty in a way that seems almost as magical as her most famous creation, Harry Potter. Although she was born into a family that was financially comfortable, as an adult Rowling went through difficult periods when she says she was very poor, but not quite homeless. In 1990, on a delayed train journey to her job in London, Rowling dreamt up the story of a young boy attending a school of wizardry. From that day on, she worked on the first *Harry Potter* book wherever she was, including Manchester, where she was a researcher, Portugal, where she taught English for 18 months, and Edinburgh, where she did a teacher training course. *Harry Potter and the Philosopher's Stone* was finished in 1995, published in 1997 – and the rest is history.

C PEP GUARDIOLA

Josep 'Pep' Guardiola, probably the most famous football coach in the world, had humble beginnings. Born in the village of Santpedor in Catalonia, Spain, his father was a builder and his mother a salesperson. He has two older sisters, and a younger brother, Pere, who is now one of the world's top football agents. Pep signed for Barcelona FC youth academy at the age of 13, and he became a member of the senior squad when he was 20. He won many titles with the club. At one point, he was coached by someone with whom he would later compete for 'most famous coach' status, José Mourinho. Pep played for Spain in two World Cups, and finished his playing career for a team in Mexico before returning to Barcelona as a coach – and his fame has continued to grow since then. He is well known not only for his tactical genius, but also for his style – he often appears in perfectly cut suits.

D JAY-Z

American rapper Jay-Z had a tough start in life, but with a combination of passion, drive and talent he has become one of the most successful rap artists in the world. He was born Shawn Corey Carter in Brooklyn, New York, the last of four children. For him, rapping was an escape from the violence and poverty of his surroundings, but his journey to success was a long one. It wasn't until he was in his 30s that he started to get really big, with his own record label and several multi-million selling albums. Always a very private individual, he seldom discusses his personal relationships, and his small wedding in 2008 to the singer Beyoncé was held in secret in his New York apartment. Jay-Z has used his money for charitable purposes, as well as investing in several businesses, including his own popular urban clothing brand.

4 **Match the highlighted words in the text to the definitions.**

1 the condition of being extremely poor ....
2 without a place to live ....
3 in or relating to the countryside ....
4 an accepted or official position, especially in a social group ....
5 attracted or interested ....

1 Choose the correct options to complete the sentences.

1 We *might enjoy / might have enjoyed* the meal if the waiter hadn't been so rude.
2 If you *had understood / understand* the question, you might have given the right answer.
3 They would have been very cold if they *didn't take / hadn't taken* their coats.
4 Maria *would have visited / will visit* more places if she had had enough time.
5 If the acting *was / had been* better, that could have been a great film.
6 If Simon *didn't get up / hadn't got up* so late, he might not have missed the bus.
7 You *wouldn't have met / wouldn't meet* your favourite actor if you hadn't gone to the theatre that evening.
8 If Mum and Dad *hadn't sold / didn't sell* our car, we might not have been able to afford a holiday.

2 Rewrite the sentences using the third conditional.

0 She didn't tell me the time of her train, so I didn't go to meet her.
   If *she had told me the time of her train, I would have gone to meet her.*
1 I didn't have lunch because I wasn't hungry.
   I
2 You told him it was a great book, so he bought it.
   If
3 He failed the test because he hadn't studied.
   He
4 Steve didn't hear about the party, so he didn't go.
   If
5 I had drunk all the milk, so Dad couldn't make a cheese sauce.
   Dad
6 Your bag was stolen because you left it outside.
   If
7 I started a new school last year and met my best friend.
   If
8 You were rude to Irina yesterday, so it isn't surprising she ignored you this morning!
   Irina

3 Complete the sentences with *I wish* and the correct form of the verbs in the box.

book	not crash	not eat	not go
have	know	phone	not spend
not stop	~~study~~	wear	

0 *I wish I had studied* harder at school.
1 _____ to bed so late last night.
2 _____ about the test.
3 _____ tickets for the Haim concert.
4 _____ so much chocolate.
5 _____ a warmer coat.
6 _____ all my money on these new trainers.
7 _____ you earlier today for a chat.
8 _____ learning to play the piano.
9 _____ the courage to say what I thought.
10 _____ my bike into the wall yesterday.

4 Correct the mistakes in five of the sentences. Which one is correct?

1 If we had took the plane, we wouldn't have seen so many interesting places.
2 If you have been there, you would enjoyed yourself!
3 Finally, I'd like to tell you that if I had known, I would have stayed at your home for the rest of my holiday.
4 I think many problems going to appear if I had bought it.
5 I really wish you were here with me last month.
6 I liked it very much and I wish you would have been able to go with me.

1 Match the phrasal verbs to their meanings.

1 get away with ....
2 get back ....
3 get into ....
4 get on with ....
5 get out of ....
6 get round to ....
7 get through ....

a avoid doing something that you don't want to do, especially by giving an excuse
b be given something again that you had before
c do something that you have intended to do for a long time
d avoid being criticised or punished for something
e succeed in, e.g., an examination or competition
f continue doing something, especially work
g be chosen or elected, e.g., for a team

2 Choose the correct words to complete the sentences.

1 Our football team has got .... to the semi-finals.
   A through   B back   C round
2 Don't lend any money to John, or you'll never get it ....
   A out   B back   C away
3 I thought I'd got .... with forgetting my homework, but the teacher remembered to ask me for it.
   A out   B through   C away
4 We've finally got .... to painting my bedroom!
   A round   B off   C through
5 I'm staying in tonight to get .... with my project.
   A on   B away   C out
6 Carmen was very happy to learn she had got .... her chosen university.
   A away   B through   C into
7 The only way you can get .... of washing the dishes is if you cook the dinner!
   A out   B away   C round

1 You are going to hear people talking in eight different situations. Read the context sentence for each question. Which recordings will only have one speaker?

1 You hear a teenager leaving a voicemail message.
   Why is she calling?
   A to apologise for missing an appointment
   B to report on an event
   C to arrange a meeting

2 You hear a young man talking to a friend about something that happened to him.
   What was he doing at the time?
   A crossing the street
   B riding a bike
   C driving a car

3 You hear two people talking about a school fair.
   What did the woman think about it?
   A There weren't enough volunteers.
   B She thought nobody enjoyed it.
   C It achieved its intended goal.

4 You overhear two friends in a shop talking about a pair of trainers.
   The friends agree that the trainers are
   A too expensive.
   B a nice colour.
   C very comfortable.

5 You overhear two friends talking about comedy.
   How did the boy first find out about the new show?
   A A friend mentioned it to him.
   B It was featured in a magazine.
   C He heard an extract online.

6 You hear a psychologist talking about her research on the subject of creativity.
   How does she feel about the way creativity is taught in schools?
   A satisfied with the results that are being produced
   B confident that her studies will improve things
   C excited by the speed of progress being made

7 You overhear a boy and a girl talking in a games shop.
   What is the girl doing?
   A recommending a game for the boy to play
   B warning the boy not to spend a lot of money
   C complaining about the boy taking too much time

8 You hear a teenage cyclist talking about his first official race.
   How does he feel?
   A surprised by the speed of the other riders
   B pleased to have done as well as he did
   C determined to train harder next time

2 Match each of the questions (1–8) in Exercise 1 to what it focuses on (a–f).

a speaker's opinion   ....
b speaker's feeling   ....
c specific information   ....
d agreement between speakers   ....
e speaker's purpose   ....
f general situation   ....

🔊 3 You will hear people talking in eight different situations.
09 For questions 1–8, choose the best answer.

19 AGAINST THE LAW

1 Complete the table with the words and phrases in the box. Some can go in more than one column.

burgle	burglar	burglary	charge	commit a crime
court	deny the charge	hacker	investigate	judge
jury	make an arrest	prisoner	release	sentence
statement	suspect	theft	victim	witness

Noun (person)	Noun (crime/other)	Verb	Phrase
		burgle	

2 Match words and phrases from Exercise 1 to the definitions.

1 someone who has suffered the effects of violence, illness or bad luck
2 get into a building illegally and steal things
3 decide and say officially the punishment for someone who has committed a crime
4 the place where a judge decides whether someone is guilty of a crime
5 the action or crime of stealing something
6 do something that is illegal
7 officially accuse someone of a crime
8 something that someone says or writes officially
9 say that you haven't done anything wrong
10 a person who sees an event happening, especially a crime or an accident
11 a group of people who listen to all the facts in a trial and decide whether a person is guilty or not guilty
12 think that someone may have committed a crime or done something bad
13 try to discover all the facts about something, especially a crime or an accident
14 a person who accesses other people's or organisations' computers illegally

3 Complete the sentences with the correct form of words from Exercise 1.

1 The police have _____ one man with the _____ of a number of bicycles from the local school.
2 Our house was _____ last night – it's the first time we've been _____ of a crime.
3 The bank robber was _____ to eight years in prison.
4 Fortunately, several _____ saw the accident and said that it wasn't my fault.
5 We are _____ the case at the moment, but haven't made an _____ yet.
6 When the case was heard in _____ yesterday, the _____ of 12 people decided the burglar was guilty, and the _____ ordered him to pay a fine.
7 Our TV, smart speaker and laptops were all stolen in the _____ .
8 Over 50% of prisoners go on to _____ more crimes after they have been _____ from prison.
9 I was shocked when I was accused of being a computer _____ – I'm useless with computers!
10 The police had reasons _____ that the man was the _____ of several other houses in the street.

1 Quickly read the article on page 77. Which of the crimes below do you think would <u>not</u> be tried in a teen court?

dropping litter
hacking into government computers
shoplifting
burglary
writing graffiti

2 Find a word in the article which means 'the person in a court who is accused of a crime'.

3 Read the article again. Are the sentences *T* (True), *F* (False) or *NM* (Not Mentioned)? Correct the false sentences. <u>Underline</u> the parts of the text which tell you the answer.

1 The people who run the teen courts are teenagers.

2 Defendants in teen courts usually deny the charges.

3 In teen courts, a jury is used to decide the sentence for serious offences.

4 A guilty offender is not allowed to take part in future court cases.

5 Victims help to decide how to punish the offenders.

6 Teen courts are successful because they help offenders understand the consequences of their actions.

7 In comparison with adult courts, teen courts tend to have a worse reoffending rate.

4 Match the highlighted words in the text to the definitions.

1 information that is stored for the future

2 suitable or right for a particular situation or occasion

3 an official plan or system

4 has an influence on someone or something

5 help or do something positive

TEEN COURTS

Teen courts are a unique and successful way of dealing with teenage criminals. Popular in the US, they provide an alternative to the traditional adult courts. Young people from the ages of 10 to 18 have their cases heard, and are sentenced at these courts – as long as their crime is not very serious.

Teen courts are run and staffed by young volunteers, who are trained in their roles by adult experts. These volunteers usually come from local high schools or youth organisations. The judge in a teen court does not usually have to decide if someone is guilty or not guilty, because most of the defendants do not deny the charges against them. The role of the teen court is simply to decide on an appropriate sentence for the crime. Sometimes the sentence is decided by a jury.

Sentences often involve the defendant being ordered to do something to help the person or people harmed by their crime. This can include writing formal apologies to the victim or doing some work to help repair damage. Another common sentence is known as 'community service', in which the offender must perform tasks which benefit the community, such as picking up litter, or helping in a care home. Often the offenders are also required to serve on a teen court jury themselves.

The whole process, from charging to sentencing, helps to bring young offenders to an understanding of their offence, and how it affects other people. They are frequently faced with the victim of their crime – an act that brings them face-to-face with the reality of what they have done. Offenders are made to feel responsible for their actions. Furthermore, by serving on a teen court jury, the offender is brought back into the system as an active member.

Simon Baxter, 16, who has been a teen court judge for two years, speaks about the success of the scheme: 'It's not about guilt or innocence or even punishment,' he says. 'It's about teenage offenders being shown the harm they've done by people their own age. It's much more powerful when people of your own age and background tell you that you did wrong, rather than adults – although the scheme does take some training to work well.'

And it does work. Evidence suggests that fewer than 5% of offenders whose cases are heard in teen courts go on to commit another crime. This compares to a 20% reoffending rate among those who go to adult courts. Not only that, teen courts also focus more on making things better for the victim, and the guilty offender does not end up with a criminal record – so everybody ends up better off in the long run.

1 Choose the correct verbs to complete the sentences.

1 You were very lucky. You *might / must* have been seriously hurt!

2 Nobody is answering the door. They *couldn't / must* have gone out.

3 The burglar *couldn't / might* have known we were on holiday, because we didn't tell anybody.

4 I'm not sure, but I think I *may / must* have forgotten to lock the front door.

5 You *couldn't / must* have heard the news! Everybody's talking about it.

6 Marie *might / can't* have forgotten about the extra practice, because I reminded her about it.

7 I don't know who phoned, but it *must / could* have been Harry.

8 It *couldn't / must* have been very cold last night because there's ice on the roads this morning.

2 Complete the conversations with a modal verb + *have* + the past participle of the verbs in brackets. Sometimes more than one modal verb is possible.

1 **A:** Thanks for all your help. I _____ (fix) the broken door without you.
   B: No problem. I think the burglar _____ (be) very strong.

2 **A:** It's possible that the police _____ (find) the criminal by now.
   B: No, they _____ (find) them yet. They don't work that fast!

3 **A:** Do you think Hunter _____ (get) stuck in traffic? He's very late.
   B: No, he _____ (get) stuck in traffic – the streets aren't busy at this time.
   A: Then you _____ (forget) to invite him. There's no other explanation!

4 **A:** I'm not sure, but I think I _____ (upset) Sophie when I told her how surprised I was that she got 100% in the test.
   B: She _____ (get) 100%. That was a really hard test. She _____ (be) lying to you.

5 **A:** Have you seen Gary recently? He's got some great news!
   B: Well, I thought I saw him at the gym yesterday evening, but it _____ (be) him, he was quite far away.
   A: No, you _____ (see) him yesterday evening, because he was with me, telling me his news.

3 Complete the second sentence so that it has a similar meaning to the first sentence. Use the word in brackets.

1 Perhaps Greg forgot to lock his bike. (might)
   Greg _____

2 I'm sure it was really frightening to find a mouse in your bedroom. (been)
   It _____

3 It's possible that they were too late for the early train. (missed)
   They _____

4 I'm certain that it wasn't a very pleasant experience. (unpleasant)
   It _____

4 Correct the mistakes in four of the sentences. Which one is correct?

1 The line-up was changed and that was the worst surprise I could have. _____

2 I spent almost an hour waiting, and then decided that the call will have been a joke. _____

3 I must have been seven years old at that time. _____

4 He could have triumph over the fish because of his knowledge of the sea. _____

5 Mark and Angela understood that he mustn't had told her the story. _____

1 Write the correct prefix to make the opposites of the adjectives.

1 ____accurate   8 ____patient
2 ____clear   9 ____polite
3 ____expensive   10 ____possible
4 ____fair   11 ____safe
5 ____honest   12 ____visible
6 ____legal   13 ____willing
7 ____organised

2 Match the prefixed adjectives from Exercise 1 to the meanings.

1 not wanting to do something _____
2 dangerous _____
3 rude _____
4 too difficult to do _____
5 likely to lie or do something criminal _____
6 against the law _____
7 not correct or exact _____
8 not able to plan things well _____
9 easily annoyed by mistakes or delays _____
10 not possible to see _____

1 Read the exam task below and answer the questions.

1 What three pieces of information should the article include?

2 Where will the article appear?

3 Can you think of a story from your own life for the article?

You see this advertisement on an international English language learning website.

> **Articles wanted**
> *Crime and punishment!*
> All children are naughty sometimes. Tell us about something naughty which you did as a child. Explain what happened, whether you were punished and how the experience affected you. The best articles will appear on our website.

2 Read the article below and put the paragraphs in the correct order.

1 .... 2 .... 3 .... 4 ....

3 Does the article include all the information from the task in Exercise 1?

....

4 Match paragraphs A–D in the article to 1–4.

1 Why I did it ....
2 What I did ....
3 Introduction ....
4 The consequences ....

5 Write your own article for the task in Exercise 1. Use your idea in Exercise 1 and the headings in Exercise 4 to help you. Write your article in 140–190 words.

Revenge gone wrong!

A As a punishment, my mother made me scrub Danny's walls clean. That was enough. She knew I felt shame about doing such a silly thing. I never tried to get anyone else into trouble again!

B Everyone does naughty things when they are a child. It's part of growing up – learning the difference between right and wrong, and finding out that we have to accept the consequences of our actions. I learned a useful lesson when I was seven years old.

C I waited until he went out. Then I went into his bedroom with a red marker pen and wrote his name on every wall, so that my parents would think it was him. Then I told my mother. Unfortunately, I must have looked very guilty because she didn't believe me. 'It can't have been Danny,' she said. 'He isn't that silly. It must have been you!'

D My older brother Danny and I had an argument. I can't remember what the argument was about, but it must have been a big one, because I was really angry with him and I wanted to get him into trouble.

VOCABULARY   Places

1 Use the clues to complete the crossword with words for places.

Across

1 the top or outside part of something
4 a soft piece of material used to cover the floor
7 a long seat for two or more people
9 a room that is below ground level in a building
10 protection from bad weather or danger
11 a hollow structure that allows the smoke from a fire inside a building to escape to the air outside
13 a place where people who live in an area can meet and play sports, take courses, etc., is called a community _____

Down

1 a small building, usually made of wood, used for storing things
2 a very hard building material
3 the basic structure of a building
5 the things that you walk on when you go up or down stairs
6 a piece of equipment used to reach high places
7 a type of fence that stops people going into an area
8 a group of buildings or rooms that are used for a particular purpose
12 a small, simple building often made of wood

2 Complete the sentences with the words in the box.

concrete   bench   ladder
complex   chimney   shed

1 The boys sat on a _____ and ate their sandwiches.
2 The new theatre is made entirely of _____, and looks really ugly.
3 My dad keeps all his tools in a _____ at the bottom of the garden.
4 Have you been to the new entertainment _____ near the park?
5 You have to climb a _____ to get into our tree house.
6 Smoke filled the room because something was blocking the _____.

3 Choose the correct words to complete the sentences.

1 That is a beautiful *basement / rug* – it's almost too nice to walk on!
2 There's a *barrier / shelter* at the end of the road to stop cars from driving down it.
3 First we built a *surface / frame*, then we threw some material over it to keep the rain out.
4 There are 20 *steps / ladders* on these stairs.
5 When it started to rain, we looked around for a *basement / shelter* – but couldn't find one.
6 We never go downstairs to the *basement / hut* in our house because it's cold and damp.
7 Be careful – the *hut / surface* of this road is slippery when it's wet.

READING

1 Quickly read the blog about teenagers and shopping malls on page 81. Choose the best title.

A The perfect teen hangout
B A revolution in shopping
C The problem of teens in shopping malls

2 The opening sentence of each paragraph has been removed from the text. Choose from sentences A–H the one which fits each gap (1–8).

A On the other hand, when a few teens do behave badly, it can mean that all of us get treated with suspicion.
B The professor also said that some towns don't have any places for teens.
C But, of course, we deal with it.
D The thing is, shopping malls have become the place for us teens to hang out.
E I don't need any money to go to the shopping mall.
F The psychology professor had something to say about that, too.
G My mother doesn't really worry too much about my choice of hangout.
H She also says that hanging out at the shopping mall is most popular in the early teens, up to about 15.

Amy's BLOG

I went to the mall at the weekend and started to think about what it means to us. You know what it's like: you ask your mum to drive you down to the shopping mall so that you can hang out with your friends and she says, 'Of course. We can do some shopping together!' Er, no, Mum. I want you to drive me to the shopping mall, and then leave me alone!

Posted 2.45 pm

1 _____ There are a number of reasons for that – we've looked at it on my psychology course. I was surfing the net for an essay when I read this quote from an article by a psychology professor at a British university: 'Adults see malls as somewhere they go to do shopping, whereas teenagers go there to socialise.'

2 _____ That's obvious – reasons being that older teens are likely to be able to go to other places: they can drive, they often have part-time jobs, so they have some money. However, for younger teens like me, the mall remains a cool place to hang out.

3 _____ No youth clubs, no parks, no safe spaces at all, which means hanging out at the mall can be an important part of teenage development. You know, a shopping mall is a safe place to meet, to talk, and to deal with the complicated issues of getting along with your friends.

4 _____ If I want to go to the swimming pool or the cinema with my friends, I need cash – and, as you can imagine, that's pretty scarce for kids my age!

5 _____ She knows I'm a fairly responsible teenager. 'If you tell me that you and your friends are always polite to the people who work there, I believe you. If you're well behaved, nobody will mind you hanging around the place too much.'

6 _____ 'Very few teenagers get into trouble at the shopping mall. But the opportunities for bad behaviour are all there. Although there is no direct adult supervision, which is what makes the place so attractive in the first place, the presence of adult shoppers and security guards does act as a controlling factor.'

7 _____ My friends and I are sometimes treated rudely by shop staff. Just because some other teenagers did some pretty awful things about a year ago, people think we're all like that. It's not exactly fair.

8 _____ Dealing with things is part of growing up, right? The main thing is that our parents understand that the shopping mall is where we go to get away from them. The last thing we want is for them to make us feel awkward in front of our friends. So, Mum, if you see me in the shopping mall, don't be surprised if I ignore you!

℀ Share 👍 Like 💬 Comment

---

3 **Match the highlighted words in the text to the definitions.**

1 difficult or causing problems or embarrassment _____
2 one of the things that has an effect on a situation _____
3 spend time enjoying yourself with other people _____
4 rare, or not available in large amounts _____
5 continues to be _____

1 Match the beginnings and ends of the sentences.

1 Choosing to study English ....
2 I really enjoy ....
3 I learnt how to cook ....
4 I never get anxious ....
5 Falling off my scooter ....
6 Sometimes I'm just not capable of ....

a was the best decision I ever made.
b from watching my dad.
c didn't hurt as much as you might think.
d about doing exams.
e watching our cats play together.
f making difficult decisions.

2 Write sentences with the words.

0 I / learn / how to play this game / by / watch / my brother
I learnt how to play this game by watching my brother.

1 Tonya / be / tired of / live / in a small house
....

2 the kids / enjoy / play / in their tree house yesterday
....

3 ride / a bike / is a good way / of / keep / fit
....

4 I / not be / capable of / fix / this computer
....

5 you shouldn't / feel / anxious about / speak / to the class
....

6 by / save / her pocket money / she was able to buy a bike
....

3 Rewrite the sentences so they start with an *-ing* form.

0 It can be dangerous to jump into the swimming pool.
Jumping into the swimming pool can be dangerous.
1 We aren't allowed to run in the corridors.
....

2 It's boring to live in the countryside.
....

3 It's useful to speak another language.
....

4 It's necessary to drive a car to get around here.
....

5 It's cool to hang out with friends at the shopping mall.
....

4 Rewrite the sentences with a suitable participle to replace the underlined words. You may need to change the word order.

0 <u>Simon was listening</u> to music and he didn't hear the phone.
Listening to music, Simon didn't hear the phone.
1 <u>When she spoke</u> to Marco, she discovered they went to the same gym.
....

2 On the way home I saw a man <u>who was sleeping</u> on a bench.
....

3 My dad's office, <u>which has</u> no air conditioning, is very hot in the summer.
....

4 <u>I felt</u> embarrassed and I left the room.
....

5 My mobile phone <u>had</u> no power and so didn't work.
....

6 Nuria <u>waited</u> for an hour for Andrea, and she wondered why she was still her friend.
....

7 I looked at all the phones and decided to buy the one <u>which offered</u> the best features.
....

8 <u>Because he didn't understand</u> one question, Eric failed the test.
....

5 Correct the mistakes in four of the sentences. Which one is correct?

1 I'm looking forward to go there.
....

2 Thank you for writing to me.
....

3 Nowadays, to go to work is a bit complicated because of the cars and the busy streets.
....

4 First of all, I think that drive 100 km on Sunday is too far.
....

5 I went out with my friends to celebrate my birthday, after have dinner in a well-known restaurant.
....

1 Match 1–8 to a–h to make compound adjectives.

1 cost-	....	**a** threatening
2 eye-	....	**b** catching
3 heart	....	**c** consuming
4 life-	....	**d** cutting
5 mouth-	....	**e** watering
6 record-	....	**f** breaking
7 time-	....	**g** warming
8 award-	....	**h** winning

2 Match the compound adjectives in Exercise 1 to their meanings.

1 causing feelings of pleasure and happiness ....

2 reducing the amount of money spent ....

3 taking up many hours ....

4 better, faster, etc., than anything before ....

5 causing danger of death ....

6 looking or smelling as if it is going to taste really good ....

7 very noticeable ....

8 having won a prize or prizes for being of high quality ....

LISTENING

1 You will hear three conversations in which people are talking about places where they used to hang out. Listen and match the conversations to the pictures.

Conversation 1 ....   Conversation 2 ....   Conversation 3 ....

2 Listen again and tick (✓) the correct column in the table.

In this conversation ...	1	2	3
a someone complains about how the place has changed.			
b they both miss going to the place.			
c someone mentions a sporting event.			
d they disagree about the cost of something.			
e a life-threatening incident is mentioned.			
f they agree that getting there was time-consuming.			

Acknowledgements

The authors and publishers acknowledge the following sources of copyright material and are grateful for the permissions granted. While every effort has been made, it has not always been possible to identify the sources of all the material used, or to trace all copyright holders. If any omissions are brought to our notice, we will be happy to include the appropriate acknowledgements on reprinting and in the next update to the digital edition, as applicable.

Key: U = Unit.

Text
U1: Text abridged from 'Tips for how to be an awesome new kid at school, by Jacinda Sicori, *The Prospect* 14/06/2013; **U8:** Text adapted from 'Are we nearly there yet? Family travels the world for 11 years' by Harriet Baskas, *NBC News* 06/04/2011; **U9:** Text adapted from 'Amazing (very) young entrepreneurs' by Nicole Fallon, *Business News Daily* 05/09/2013 Copyrighted 2014. TechMedia Network. 112843:1114AT; **U16:** Text adapted from 'Top ten surprising results of global warming', by Live Science staff, *Live Science* 16/10/2011 Copyrighted 2014. TechMedia Network. 113255:1114AT; **U17:** Text adapted from 'Has Banksy's real identity been discovered at last?' by Robert Verkaik, *The Independent* 14/07/2008.

Photography
The following images are sourced from Getty Images.

U1: mixetto/E+; FatCamera/E+; Hero Images; **U2**: Steve Prezant/Image Source; Klaus Vedfelt/Taxi; **U3**: Lester Cohen/Getty Images Entertainment; Harry How/Getty Images Sport; Bettmann; Patrick Branwell Bronte/Getty; Westend61; Imgorthand/E+; **U4**: Marco Zollino/EyeEm; agmit/E+; shayes17/E+; Escaflowne/E+; SDubi/iStock/Getty Images Plus; **U5**: Tim Hall/Cultura; Hero Images; **U6**: Maskot; Hero Images; JackF/iStock/Getty Images Plus; **U7**: Eva-Katalin/E+; Ernesto r. Ageitos/Moment; **U8**: FatCamera/E+; Glowimages; **U9**: ballda/iStock/Getty Images Plus; DronG/iStock/Getty Images Plus; Khatawut Chaemchamras/EyeEm; DmyTo/iStock/Getty Images Plus; monticelllo/iStock/Getty Images Plus; Westend61; bilgehan yilmaz/iStock/Getty Images Plus; OktalStudio; bilgehan yilmaz/iStock/Getty Images Plus; **U10**: RapidEye/E+; South_agency/E+; Caiaimage/Tom Merton; Alexander Kirch/EyeEm; **U11**: Ani_Ka/DigitalVision Vectors; hudiemm/DigitalVision Vectors; AndreyTTL/E+; Science & Society Picture Library/SSPL; GrapeImage/E+; Dinoco Greco/PhotoAlto Agency RF Collections; **U12**: kali9/E+; Ababsolutum/E+; Westend61; **U13**: Dmytro Aksonov/E+; John Weast/Getty Images Sport; **U14**: RapidEye/Vetta; Nigel Killeen/Moment; **U15**: MiMaLeFi/iStock/Getty Images Plus; asiseeit/E+; fStop Images - Andreas Stamm/Brand X Pictures; **U16**: Gleb Tarro/Moment; Sam Antonio; Photography/Moment; Michael Heim/EyeEm; Photo by Stuart Gleave/Moment; Pete Saloutos; Vasily Popov/500Px Plus; Simon Ritzmann/Photodisc; **U17:** Manchan/Photodisc; Alessandro Salvador/EyeEm; Maxlevoyou/E+; **U18:** J. Countess/Getty Images News; Athena Pictures/Getty Images Sport; Cindy Ord/Getty Images Entertainment; Taylor Hill/FilmMagic; **U19:** Image Source; skynesher/E+; **U20:** Comstock/Stockbyte; Tassii/E+; FatCamera/E+.

The following photographs have been sourced from other library/sources.

U8: Courtesy of Zapp family; **U17:** Lewis Tse Pui Lung/Shutterstock; **U19:** ZUMA Press, Inc/Alamy Stock Photo.

Front cover photography by oxygen/Moment/Getty Images.

Illustration
Kevin Hopgood (Beehive Illustration); Mark Duffin; Rory Walker.

The publishers are grateful to the following contributors: cover design and design concept: restless; typesetting: emc design Ltd; audio recordings: produced by Leon Chambers and recorded at The SoundHouse Studios, London; project management: Carol Goodwright